Praise for *We, Robots*

Praise for Curtis White

ALSO BY CURTIS WHITE

NONFICTION

Monstrous Possibility: An Invitation to Literary Politics

The Middle Mind: Why Americans Don't Think for Themselves

*The Spirit of Disobedience: Resisting the Charms of Fake Politics,
    Mindless Consumption, and the Culture of Total Work*

The Barbaric Heart: Faith, Money, and the Crisis of Nature

*The Science Delusion: Asking the Big Questions in a Culture of Easy
    Answers*

FICTION

Heretical Songs

Metaphysics in the Midwest

The Idea of Home

Anarcho-Hindu

Memories of My Father Watching TV

Requiem

America's Magic Mountain

WE, ROBOTS

ROBOTS

Staying Human in the Age of Big Data

CURTIS WHITE

 MELVILLE HOUSE
BROOKLYN · LONDON

WE, ROBOTS

Portions of this book have appeared in *Playboy*, *Lapham's Quarterly*, *Tricycle*, *Jacobin*, *The Village Voice*, and *The Big Other*.

Melville House Publishing   8 Blackstock Mews
            46 John Street   and Islington
        Brooklyn, NY 11201   London N4 2BT

mhpbooks.com   facebook.com/mhpbooks   @melvillehouse

Paperback ISBN: 978-1-61219-610-7

The Library of Congress has cataloged the hardcover as follows:
White, Curtis, 1951– author.
    We, robots : staying human in the age of big data / Curtis White.
    pages   cm
    ISBN 978-1-61219-455-4 (hardback)
    ISBN 978-1-61219-456-1 (ebook)
    1. Human beings.   2. Philosophical anthropology.   I. Title.

BD450.W493 2015
128—dc23
                                            2015032089

Design by Marina Drukman

Printed in the United States of America
1   3   5   7   9   10   8   6   4   2

There was a time when humanity faced the universe alone and without a friend. Now he has creatures to help him; stronger creatures than himself, more faithful, more useful, and absolutely devoted to him. Mankind is no longer alone.

—Isaac Asimov, *I, Robot*

We must realize that modern civilization is thoroughly oriented towards dehumanizing humanity in every possible way; that is to say, we are fast turning into robots or statues with no human souls. Our task is to get humanized once more.

—D. T. Suzuki

CONTENTS

Introduction
THE PHILOSOPHY
OF AS-IF

Man is a make-believe animal—he is never so truly himself as when he is acting a part.

—William Hazlitt

Isn't it amazing how often a doctor will live up to our expectation of how a doctor should look?

—*My Dinner with Andre*

When I was an undergraduate studying philosophy at the University of San Francisco in the late sixties, I discovered Hans Vaihinger and his *Philosophy of As-If* (originally "The Theory of Scientific Fictions"), developed between 1876 and 1911.

"The consciously false," Vaihinger wrote, "plays an enormous part in science, in philosophies, and in life."

> I wanted to give a complete enumeration of all the methods in which we operate intentionally with consciously false ideas . . . It must be remembered that the purpose of the world of ideas as a whole is not the portrayal of reality—this would be an utterly impossible task—but to provide us with an *instrument for finding our way about more easily in this world.*

For Vaihinger, our ideas are not a picture or copy of the actual world; they are used only to deal with an otherwise unknowable reality. We live in a parallel world of our own making far more than we live in "reality." He liberally quotes Friedrich Nietzsche, who wrote in *Human, All Too Human*: "The significance of language for the evolution of culture lies in this, that mankind set up in language a separate world beside the other world, a place it took to be so firmly set that, standing upon it, it could lift the rest of the world off its hinges and make itself master of it."

What was behind this parallel world of stories? For Vaihinger, the answer was science. Charles Darwin, for example, told a story about the origins of modern species that was broadly believed until very recently. He argued that all species are linked to their ancient ancestors in the same way that the branches of a tree are connected. Thus, the metaphor of the great Tree of Life, on which living species are all on the upper most limbs and the extinct ancestor species are farther down the trunk. For the branch *homo sapiens*, there is the descending branch of the Neanderthals, who evolved from the Asian *homo erectus*, who were begat by the ape-man *Australopithecus*. This story provided narrative stability for scientists (if not Christians) until the recent discovery of many more *hominin* strains complicated the matter. But for Vaihinger, even if stories like Darwin's are false they still contribute to our species' ability to adapt, thrive, and evolve. In other words, they are useful.

As Vaihinger wrote aphoristically, "What we call *truth* is really only the most expedient form of error."*

Vaihinger also observed something he called the "law of the preponderance of the means over the end." At some point in our development, our stories began to take on a life of their own that came to seem even more important than the practical purposes they were originally intended to serve. It is this "preponderance of means," and not mere survival, that makes life "worth living," as we humans say. Darwin may have understood the struggle for life, but he had little to say about the quality of life. In the end, we don't want to survive under just any terms: we want meaning, richness, satisfaction, happiness, wisdom, *all* of it.

This "preponderance" has manifested itself in ways that are so familiar to us that we forget to marvel at how richly superfluous they are. Consider sex (as I'm sure you have). Animals copulate and animals breed, but unlike the other beasts humans spend much of their lives seeking something they call romantic

---

* Vaihinger takes this from Friedrich Schiller, who wrote, "In error only is there life; and knowledge must be death."

love. Some lovers are richly satisfied, or sated, or wounded, or homicidally enraged by the desires romantic longing produces. There is bliss, fistfights with rivals, rapture, and broken china. Some feel that by falling in love they have become whole for the first time while others claim they are permanently damaged (and sometimes both). There are unforgettable memories of a weekend in Capri (or the basement sofa when the parents were out), and there are those contrary days when an irate spouse has had the lock on the front door replaced and a court order issued barring the other from their home. Sexual reproduction may be the Darwinian theme, but it is like the banal melody by Diabelli that Beethoven turned into magical and infinite variations, some full of confident energy, some melancholy, and some both by turns.

As with the notorious French person who would never have fallen in love if she hadn't read about it first, our "sex lives," as we say, are not something apart from what we find in art. For instance, in Marcel Proust's *Swann's Way*, Swann is in love with Odette but the only thing he really knows about her is that she reminds him of a painting and a beautiful melody. This does nothing to prepare him for the discovery that she likes to hide behind boulders with other girls, where, Swann must imagine, the alarming creatures do God knows what. Like Swann, it is often difficult for us to know if what we are in love with is a human being or something we read about in D. H. Lawrence, viewed in *Casablanca*, or saw on the pages of *Cosmopolitan* or—for those who don't need much encouragement—in an Yves St. Laurent underwear advertisement. It seems that only our stories make our aboriginal grunting and spilling of seed worthy of our interest.*

And, revealingly, our thinking about the sex act itself is narrative: it has a ground situation (foreplay), rising action (if you will), crisis (that delicious just-before), climax (*if* you will), and denouement (what the French [for some reason] call the little death, *petite mort*), all of it delightfully whipped up in "concupiscent curds," in Wallace Stevens's phrase. Even the human body itself seems an expression of the "preponderance of means": we're not just sex organs, not genitals, not just *lingam* and *yonni*. Every part of the body is capable of being a "secondary sexual characteristic," largely because we frame those parts seductively—a swollen bicep, a turned ankle, a scapular revealed by a loose blouse. There are even display-of-secondary-sex-characteristics artists, like flamingo or belly dancers, yielding gracefully to the encouragement of castanet or *tabla*.

The same sort of thing is true of food. Given the choice, no human being eats "food." For us, there is no such thing. A horse may have his bag of oats, but that's not how we roll. Nor do we merely consume calories and nutrients (triathletes noted and duly excepted). Humans have cuisines—Italian, French, Cajun,

---

* François Rabelais's opinion was that the whole thing was disgusting and that no one would ever have sex if they weren't like the dancing brown dumplings in Pieter Breugel's peasant paintings: drunk.

Thai, as well as hybrids like Cuban-Chinese found in that exotic land called the Upper West Side—and they have heady vintages, a brave new world of craft beers, food-porn on TV, and the gaudy world of sugar and fat we call dessert. In short, human beings are not Darwinian survivalists, they are maximalists. What makes the maximalizing of our cultures possible is our playfulness and our narrative inventions, which are distillations of play. Every recipe is a story about the refinement of taste.

I had two reactions to reading Vaihinger. First, I wondered if his modest suggestions qualified as philosophy at all. I was used to the titans of thought like Descartes, Kant, and Hegel who developed universal systems based upon elaborate truth claims (*science*, as they understood it). But Vaihinger seemed only to be telling me about how to understand truth claims, not making one himself (except insofar as he might have been saying that the only truth is that there is no truth).

My second reaction was that, of course, he was right. For a young man in San Francisco in 1969, the world seemed to be only about the ruthless critique of everything we had thought to be true—beginning with the lies of parents, politicians, and the purveyors of science at Dow, Monsanto, and Lockheed—and the replacement of those lies with our own creations. In other words, we replaced official lies with art—the Beatles, and psychedelia at the top of the list. We took care to acknowledge frankly that our art creations were made up, were fictions. In fact, the made-up-ness of our creations was the point: we were after the open and endless freedom of self-creation (the Diggers called it "free frame of reference"), something we deeply preferred to the social roles that had been provided for us by "bow-tie daddy" and the "brain police" as The Mothers of Invention put it. We would be unlike our fathers and mothers and unlike what Jean-Luc Godard investigates in his 2010 *Film Socialisme*:

> There's a character, the Mother, who could care less if she has a life, if life is considered an end in itself. She doesn't have the slightest doubt that she is alive. It never occurs to her to wonder how and why or in what way she is. In short, she is not aware of being a character, because she has never, not even for a moment, been detached from her role. She doesn't know she has a role.

Yet that's exactly what we knew: that we were supposed to inhabit roles. But San Francisco was, for a blessed time, a Vaihingerian City of Fabulists. We put on masks but did not ask anyone to submit to them. Instead, we pointed to them ourselves, in confession, not pretending that the masks were in any sense true. Over in the Castro District, gay men and lesbians were destroying hetero-normalcy through the invention of new sexes: leather sex, feather sex, motorcycle sex, cowboy sex, and, most flamboyant of all, the transcendental gender atrocities of the queer vaudeville act known as the Cockettes. No one thought that they were establishing a new truth about sex; the point was that this self-creation of sexual identities was never-ending. (That was the gay community's lesson to *all* of us, maybe especially the resolutely hetero-normal.) Human life was supposed to be about *becoming*, and not about taking whatever role the world had in mind for you. This seemed at the time a healthier, freer, less repressive way of going about the business of life, and it definitely seemed a lot less likely to lead to the jungles of Vietnam.

But there are important things missing in Vaihinger. Most important, in his telling, the dissemination of a culture's stories is homogeneous and evenly spread throughout a culture because he seems to have assumed that cultures themselves are homogenous. This was so because he believed that the sources of our stories are biology and evolution, not the corridors of power or the corporate boardroom, and certainly not the Left Bank or the Haight. For Vaihinger, our as-ifs (stories about what capitalism is, what religion is, what gender is, what success is, etc.) were only about what evolutionary scientists call "adaptive fitness," not freedom.

The second thing missing in Vaihinger is familiarity with the professional storytellers—poets, writers, musicians, and artists. In spite of his heretical views on the nature of scientific truth, and in spite of the fact that his philosophy was based on fiction-making, Vaihinger was curiously silent on the importance of art. Unfortunately, this meant that he was unaware that novelists in particular had long before arrived at his conclusions. This was especially true for a tradition in the novel—a tradition I came to embrace as a writer of fiction—that begins with that great French iconoclast François Rabelais.

In Part One of this book, I will try to make amends for what's missing in Vaihinger and address some of the most seductive tales spun by some of our most powerful storytellers: libertarian economists, science writers, ecologists, city planners, and more. The stories they tell are all as-ifs that won't admit the fact. They speak of their stories only as rational, empirical, and realistic. This, too, is a story—one that is particularly dangerous. My consistent claim will be that their stories have two things in common: a fervid belief in free-market capitalism, and a habit of thinking that everything is about machines and mechanisms. In short, a world conceived through robots.

In Part Two, I will turn to the great alternative to the scientific worldview. This alternative is a *tradition* that is at present mostly oppressed but that stretches from Rabelais in the sixteenth century to the present. It is the "other side of the story," so to speak. It is the tradition of the "preponderance of means" in which the as-if-ness of our stories is elaborated in an ongoing "ode to joy," as Schiller and through him Beethoven thought of it. These are the stories of Vaihinger's children: the artists and philosophers of Play.

Part One
IDEOLOGY TODAY

What I claim is to live to the full the contradictions of my time, which may well make sarcasm the condition of truth.

—ROLAND BARTHES, *Mythologies*

I would prefer that nothing were true, rather than know that *you* were right, that *your* truth turned out to be right.

—NIETZSCHE

Like a motley assortment of zombies—some dressed in top hat and spats, some in jodhpurs, some more hardscrabble with a Cargill seed cap, others in Wall Street black with a white scrim of coke around the nostrils—the ideological narratives of the past surround us. Upper-crust, "right sort" elitism? Check. Evangelical dumb bunnies? Got 'em. Galilean mechanical determinists? All too present. Age-old stereotypes about race/class/gender? Oh, yeah. Protestant work ethic? Present as ever like a starched white collar or a noose around our necks. The selfishness-is-good crowd? You bet. The Big Swinging D*cks are all junked up and ready to build a book.* The myths of nationalism are also still with us in their ever undead way. Even Barack Obama contributes to their survival, as he did in his 2012 nomination acceptance speech: "Every day they make me proud. Every day they remind me how blessed we are to live in the greatest nation on earth."

While these stories are still present, they are mostly irrelevant, history's freak show sitting in circus boxcars on a rail siding. That is, they don't have much to contribute to the creation of new stories that have a probable claim to the future—the inevitable future, as it is usually put. There is something newish about the storytellers as well. There is nothing avuncular about them, they're freshly shrink-wrapped and barcoded: libertarian economists like Tyler Cowen; techno-gurus at Google; New Atheist rationalists like Michael Shermer writing for *Scientific American*; even polished documentary storytellers like the filmmaker Ken Burns—all of these have contributions to make to the re-narration of the present.

What follows is mostly concerned not with those fabrications that have been with us for the last two centuries—God, morality, patriotism, the Founding Fathers, military heroism, the "bitch goddess" success—but with our new storytellers, the masters of tomorrow. Whether in science, technology, or economics, these stories are being rapidly naturalized and made to seem

---

* My loose translation is: "The biggest traders are excited about enlarging their investment portfolios."

inevitable. "And so what?" some might ask. "It's all about human curiosity and creativity, isn't it, and what's wrong with that?"

At a minimum, there are two things wrong. The first is obvious: our new stories have a strong tendency to stabilize a world arranged according to the needs of techno-capitalism. The second is more subtle: they all involve the assumption that everything can be explained in mechanistic terms, that everything is, in a sense, robotic. And so I have organized the sections of Part One under five different kinds of robot: the Money-Bot, the STEM-Bot, the Buddha-Bot, the Eco-Bot, and the Art-Bot. These correspond to the techno-rationality through which we currently view the economy, science, spirituality, nature, and art.

Concerning the style in which Part One is written, I have tried not to write a book that resembles the kind of books that critics are expected to write—"serious," sober, straight-faced, linear, a little bit scholarly—when engaging "current affairs." I pause often in order to laugh. As Marshall McLuhan noted in the preface to *The Mechanical Bride*, he wrote the book as an "amusement." He continues:

> Many who are accustomed to the note of moral indignation will mistake this amusement for mere indifference. But the time for anger and protest is in the early stages of a new process. The present state is extremely advanced.

Indeed, our situation is advanced. Nothing discussed here is a threat that we will have to confront in the future. It's all here now. But what is here now still needs, moment by moment, to gain our consent, and it does that by telling us stories—most of which are effective even if they are also laughably false. What we should want to know now is not whether the techno-plutocracy of the present can be reversed, because it cannot. There's no going back. There's nothing back there to go to (assuming you're not a right-wing nationalist). What we should want to know is if it is too late to move forward by telling different stories. Once we know how silly are the stories we currently live under—once we have *laughed* at them—we can declare our independence from them and do what artists do: claim the human freedom to be the creators of their own world. The artists wait for us to join them. Romantic poets, symbolists, cubists, twelve-tone composers, modernist avant-gardists, beatniks, free jazz boppers, hippies, writers of postmodern fiction, punks, hip-hoppers, and every manner of indie rock band, these are all social movements first, social movements offered through art.

Unlike much socialist thought, art does not ask that we sacrifice living now in the name of some distant time when victory has been won. Art is part of a politics of refusal. What is gratifying about the politics of art and counterculture is that we get to live our resistance now through play, beauty, laughter, and the promise of happiness. *Through art we learn what we want.* We learn what we mean by "freedom." And we are inoculated against not only the techno-capitalist present but against the disappointments of the "perfected" socialist state. By beginning through art and philosophy, we are much less likely to be "fooled again," as The Who sang, by either capitalists or socialists.

Some of the chapters here are long and some are quite short. They are fragmented, discontinuous, and written in many voices ranging from the analytical to the satirical to the (sparingly, I hope) silly. Some are what I think of as "socialist prose poems." *We, Robots* is not written in the unified voice of the scholar, the journalist, the satirist, or the professional pundit, although it would be easy to find aspects of all of these. If it should remind you of anything in particular, it might be Nietzsche's gay science of the "free spirit." This book also has honored antecedents like Roland Barthes's *Mythologies* and McLuhan's *The Mechanical Bride*. But for the most part I simply try to practice what I preach: to create counter-narratives and suggest alternative cultures all through the supreme seriousness of that most exasperated plurality, the human freedom to create its own world. This is a *serious* book, therefore it must *play*.

By which I mean to say that this book, too, is an As-If, a confession, a health-giving fiction, and, in short, the liberatory practice of art.

#Money-Bot

SEND IN THE CLONES

In the early 1970s, I started playing chess with two of my professors at the University of San Francisco. I was a novice and they were low-level club players. They beat me regularly, of course, although through sheer force of intellectual will I was sometimes able to entertain them for one game. After that, it was like asking an infantryman, fallen on the field of honor, to get up and fight the next battle.

Being a person with an occasionally combative disposition, I was tempted by these defeats to take the game more seriously, and I did begin to learn basic openings and tactics. But then one day after a late morning of play in a Golden Gate Park bower, one of my friends turned to me and said, "Curt, it's okay to take this game seriously but only after you're sure that there's nothing important left to do."

This friend was an older poet and someone whose intuitions about life I trusted without hesitation, and this advice struck me immediately as being the truth. I was only twenty-three and I had in no way concluded that I'd done everything—or anything!—and so my interest in chess faded away.

I start with this anecdote because it is such a strong contrast to what we are now being told by economists like Tyler Cowen—in his recent book *Average Is Over: Powering America Beyond the Age of the Great Stagnation*—and by conservative pundits like *New York Times* columnist David Brooks. They argue that in some ways chess—especially chess played in the company of "intelligent machines"—is the *most* important, *most* serious, and *most* consequential thing that will happen in a person's life now and into the foreseeable future.

But first, let me back up a little.

The story that Cowen and others offer for our consumption is this: "In the future, most jobs will be performed by robots, or 'intelligent machines.'" This story is being told and repeated by Cowen and others in order to create a sense of inevitability. We are also being told that there is nothing unjust about the world universal robotics will bring because it will reward the most deserving among us: the talented, the intelligent, the well-educated, and the creative who are capable of working with robots. In short, the robotic economy of the future is coming and there's nothing you can do about it. Nor should you want to, because it is just.* Yes, there will be winners and losers, but that's

---

* In a 2014 "Economic Scene" column in *The New York Times*, Eduardo Porter commented about tech-driven economic inequality: "Some find support in the ant and the grasshopper. As one reader articulated in a recent e-mail: 'Those who deserve to be poor should be

the American way, the entrepreneurial spirit: stand on your own two feet, to the winners go the spoils, and the rest of the hoary folktales of our winner-take-all society. Folktales or not, we are asked to consent to them and accept yet another version of what sixteenth-century philosopher Etienne de la Boétie first called "voluntary servitude."

As we know well enough, there is no shortage of evidence that this "economy of the future" is not only coming but already here. (As William Gibson is reputed to have said, "The future is with us, it's just unevenly distributed.") Take the poor travel agent, rendered irrelevant in the age of Expedia: Jamaica's giant tourist warehouses and the Caribbean's cruise ship metropoles now seem to fill up by themselves. Similarly, Google Compare and Compare Now will soon do the same for many insurance agents—i.e., turn them out of their jobs. Many of our factories have been emptied out, except for roving teams of IT geeks running diagnostic apps and replacing the occasional fried semiconductor. And soon we won't even have to drive the cars that the robots build: Google will program bulked-up Siris to do that for us. Even yours truly, hunched over his laptop composing this sentence, has reason to worry: algorithms created by companies like Narrative Science are writing more and more of the reports we read, whether summaries of high school baseball games or prose condensations of the numbers provided by Big Data.

---

poor. Those who desire to be rich should be rich. That is what justice looks like.'" Porter did not approve of this chilling attitude—he was only acknowledging that it was out there.

And professors? MOOCs (massive online open courses) will teach thousands at a time, "democratizing" education and ridding the world of a lot of super-smug experts, saving taxpayers money, and delivering the coup de grâce to tenure, already vestigial from decades of attrition. What few professors remain will have "evolved," per Cowen, to be "more like athletic coaches, personal therapists, and preachers." They will not be scholars; they will be "motivators."* Even scientists will have to adjust. Because of the complexity of the quantum universe, the science of the future will not be a realm for science heroes like Newton and Einstein but for "machine science," an elaborate bureaucracy in which, as Cowen says, "*no one* understands the equations." Like the drones in Terry Gilliam's *Brazil*, they may not even be able to understand the bureaucratic machines in which they work.

But what about the titans of Wall Street? Surely they're safe. But no, not even the masters of the universe will be masterful, because algorithms will do ever more of the trading and with fewer errors made by hapless fuckups like Howie Hubler, the Morgan Stanley trader who cost the company $9,000,000,000 in a Credit Default Swap gone terribly wrong.

In this hyper-automated era, products will be abundant and cheap, profits will be higher because of machine efficiencies,

---

* Future motivator-scholars will be happy to learn that there is now a science of motivation from which they can learn their new occupation. According to Gabriele Oettingen, author of *Rethinking Positive Thinking: Inside the New Science of Motivation*, this science has already discovered that "positive thinking" doesn't work (it induces complacency). Imagining the obstacles between you and your goals works better. In other words, pessimism works. Perhaps at long last the world is ready for Schopenhauer.

and, best of all, the robots won't demand overtime pay or join unions. And they certainly won't need to take a coffee break or a piss. The ideological gurus of this world, the next wave of World Thinkers vying to knock Richard Dawkins from the podium, will be people like Cowen. (His title phrase—"average is over"—has become so familiar so quickly that pundits like Thomas Friedman use it without attribution, as if to say that the term is common currency and even common sense.) But Cowen is hardly alone. Prominent among his companions are Erik Brynjolfsson and Andrew McAfee (*Race Against the Machine*, and *The Second Machine Age*); Martin Ford (*The Lights in the Tunnel*); Ray Kurzweil (*The Age of Intelligent Machines*, and *The Singularity Is Near*); all the excitable folks at *Wired Magazine*, especially Kevin Kelly and his controversial *Wired* essay "Better than Human: Why Robots Will—and Must—Take Our Jobs"; and (this shouldn't surprise you) the aforementioned robot-cheerleader-in-chief David Brooks. Strikingly, in spite of the frightening prospect for future employment (or lack thereof) that these books and essays anticipate, all these writers call themselves "optimists."

At first glance, there doesn't seem to be much room for optimism: the recovery from the 2008 recession was famously jobless in large part because most of the jobs that paid middle-class salaries were not refilled, and they weren't refilled because economizing employers realized that the humans in these positions were expensive and/or not very productive to begin with, so companies invested in technologies to replace them. As a consequence, we have seen the sad spectacle of unemployed middle management and outmoded tech workers (low-level data drones and their supervisors) unable to reenter the workforce in their former jobs and at their former salaries. These workers have found themselves in the discouraging position of having to compete with high school kids and underclass minorities for jobs flipping burgers at Wendy's, or competing with philosophy PhDs and the latest arrivals from Somalia to drive a taxi. Unfortunately, in the Uber era, neither philosopher, Somali, nor economic refugee will find long-term refuge driving a hack. In other words, those fortunate enough to survive the seismic disruptions of the robot economy are, smartphones in hand, perfectly capable of getting around town without a taxi. Meanwhile, there go thousands of working-class jobs along with attendant dreams of middle-class security. All this suffering has been well documented—its main function now is to provide anecdotal evidence of our recent recession—and we all feel the pain of the displaced and the dispossessed because it's pretty obvious that there but for the grace of God we go.

To view the situation with a more dispassionate eye, there are the quietly devastating statistical conclusions of the Department of Labor's monthly jobs reports. According to an oft-cited *AP* analysis of employment trends since the recession:

> In the United States, half the 7.5 million jobs lost during the Great Recession were in industries that pay middle-class wages, ranging from $38,000 to $68,000. But only 2 percent of the 3.5 million jobs gained since the recession ended

in June 2009 are in midpay industries. Nearly 70 percent are in low-pay industries.

AP offers the following example:

> Webb Wheel Products makes parts for truck brakes, which involves plenty of repetitive work. Its newest employee is the Doosan V550M, and it's a marvel. It can spin a 130-pound brake drum like a child's top, smooth its metal surface, then drill holes—all without missing a beat. And it doesn't take vacations or "complain about anything," says Dwayne Ricketts, president of the Cullman, Ala., company.
>
> Thanks to computerized machines, Webb Wheel hasn't added a factory worker in three years, though it's making 300,000 more drums annually, a 25 percent increase.

Now, as any economic historian can tell you, there is nothing new in this; we could just as easily be talking about the prospect of wool knitting machines replacing members of the hand-knitters guild in 1589 (Queen Elizabeth forbade this particular innovation: she was worried that all the stocking knitters would become beggars). What's different is that in the past skilled workers were replaced with unskilled workers taught to operate machines (de-skilling), but in the present situation a small number of highly educated and hyper-skilled workers (geeks, techies) are replacing slightly less skilled middle-class workers who are being driven down into the population of unskilled labor. A successful supervisor of an office full of systems analysts in 1995 could find to her horror in 2013 that the systems are now perfectly capable of analyzing themselves and require no supervision; that she is for that reason now without marketable skills; and that—the thought is dizzying—she is for the first time a member of that surplus population that Marx called the *lumpenproletariat,* a formless mass of people who are simply not needed. Perhaps this is just the creative destruction of the market at work once again, but it ought at least to be seen for the brutal thing that it is.

Cowen, too, predicts that it's going to get worse because the adaptation of intelligent machines to the world of work is, believe it or not, in an early stage.[2] Machine intelligence gets better and invades more job categories with every year. In the age of the nanny-bot, even the teenager living two doors down the street is in danger of losing her babysitting gig.

He writes:

> [W]orkers more and more will come to be classified into two categories. The key questions will be: Are you good at working with intelligent machines or not? Are your skills a complement to the skills of the computer, or is the computer doing better without you? Worst of all, are you *competing against* the computer?

Of course, in the world that Cowen imagines, there will be winners and losers, and it is his grim responsibility to tell us who they are likely to be. At the top of the heap will be the 10 to 15 percent who have learned how to work with intelligent machines. These are the so-called "freestylers" who are capable of symbiosis with computers. This is where chess comes in, because Cowen's leading example of the economic actor most likely to prosper will be someone like the chess player who has learned to play *with* the computer. The best chess player in the world is not a Russian, and it is not IBM's celebrated Deep Blue; the best chess player is a man-bot, a Russian with a computer processing 200,000 positions per second and whispering its conclusions in his ear. The Russian then does his best to sort it all out and use his experience and intuition (what's left of it) to make a move.

Like this chess player, the best and most highly compensated workers will be freestylers who can complement machine intelligence in Silicon Valley, Wall Street, and the local factory that once employed 10,000 people but now needs only a staff of thirty. (In *Who Owns the Future?* Jaron Lanier gives the example of Kodak, which once employed 140,000 people, as opposed to Instagram, which employed only thirteen when it was taken over by Facebook—for $1 billion—in 2012.)

In a 2014 article for *Wired*, Felix Salmon fully agrees:

> It's increasingly clear that for smart organizations, living by numbers alone simply won't work. That's why they arrive at . . . synthesis—the practice of marrying quantitative insights with old-fashioned subjective experience. [C]onsider weather forecasting: The National Weather Service employs meteorologists who, understanding the dynamics of weather systems, can improve forecasts by as much as 25 percent compared with computers alone. A similar synthesis holds in economic forecasting: Adding human judgment to statistical methods makes results roughly 15 percent more accurate.

Commentators like Salmon have so saturated the media and have encountered so little resistance that their claims are close to taken for granted. *Of course* robots will do most work in the future. Their ascendance is inevitable, and the cyborg era is an anonymous force, with no relation to political economy. This inevitable era would seem to be something like the weather, and writers like Cowen are weather vanes we need in order to tell which way the wind blows. (Apologies to Dylan.) When a political project can pass as a fact of nature, it is the sign of a highly successful piece of ideology.

So don't scold your kids when they spend the day playing chess with computers, and certainly don't tell them that there are more important things they should do first, as my professor advised me. Your kids won't get away with that sort of lax thinking these days: playing chess against or with a computer may be the most important job training they will ever receive.

Cowen concludes his presentation of freestyling thusly:

> If you and your skills are a complement to the computer, your wage and labor market prospects are likely to be cheery. If your skills do not complement the computer, you may want to address that mismatch.

Perhaps Cowen means this as a word to the wise, but it sounds a little threatening to me.*

---

* Cowen ignores one old-fashioned sector of the economy: established wealth. The already-wealthy will continue to do well in the economy of the future. The top 1 percent of the top 1 percent will continue to benefit from outrageous executive pay, an underregulated financial sector, and reduced tax "incidence" for the wealthiest. (Incidence is the actual tax level after deductions and other maneuvers like doing your banking in Luxembourg.) Cowen would have us believe that the economy of the future will be distorted by a "skills bias"; but in an economy where the top .01 percent earn an income share over 6 percent, there is a much greater wealth bias. So we might want to add the following to Cowen's dictum: "If you are already wealthy, your prospects are cheery. If you're not wealthy, you might want to address that mismatch."
Get on it!

•

So OK I'm an automaton, what the hell?

—SLAVOJ ŽIŽEK

•

INTRODUCING THE ENTOURAGE ECONOMY

So, that's the elite of the near future. And what does Cowen see for those in the middle? In a word, marketing! *Self*-marketing! Self-*branding*! He writes: "Despite all the talk about STEM fields, I see *marketing* as the seminal sector of our future economy." Which means, for him, job growth in personal services. The marketing will be about you promoting your services to the high earners. Maids, chauffeurs, gardeners. Personal trainers, private tutors, nannies, interior designers, classy sex workers. These jobs will be available for the talented and the motivated because of the following:

> At some point it is hard to sell more physical stuff to high earners, yet there is usually just a bit more room to make them feel better. Better about the world. Better about themselves. Better about what they have achieved.

Even economists from a very different part of the political spectrum (Cowen self-describes as conservative and libertarian) mostly agree with Cowen's account, even if they don't agree with his conclusions. Writing for *Pieria*, economics writer Frances Coppola has this to say about how automation is changing the world of work in the service sector:

Giving someone your undivided attention for an hour is an incredibly valuable gift. Combining that with a skill in some form of "grooming"—hairdressing, manicure, massage and the like—enables you to charge for what essentially is a social bonding activity. The same is true of the various "personal development" industries—counseling, personal training, personal shopping, image consultancy—and of course the caring industries.

The long and short of this is that what survives of the middle class in the future will be a servant class. A class of motivators. A class of sycophants, whose jobs will depend not only on their skills but on their ability to flatter and provide pleasure for elites. As David Brooks sees it, this will be a class of "greeters" (a cruel piece of nomenclature), people with a "capacity for high-end service . . . and flattery." Call this the "Entourage Economy." Your masseuse has got your back.*

The Entourage Economy will not be limited to marketing professional services. Even the most private aspects of our lives will be available for rent: our cars, our homes, and ourselves. This is the shiny new "sharing economy" where not only can you profitably rent your car (Lyft), your house (Airbnb), and your swap-willing spouse (Tinder), you can also sign up on

---

* As usual, there will be greeters and there will be super-greeters. If you are fortunate enough to be coaching a member of the top .01 percent, your compensation can be equal to that of the 1 percent. For example, Marshall Goldsmith—whose clients include Ford CEO Alan Mulally—charges $25,000 for a one-day coaching seminar.

The self-pampering of the moneyed class seems to know few limits. The rich can now consult "financial therapists" when they become anxious about their financial condition. Part therapist and part adviser, financial therapists charge $2,000 per hour at the upper end, but claim that they can achieve clarity and calm for their clients. They do not take pro-bono cases for people who are stressed about not having any money at all.

TaskRabbit and rent yourself out as a high-tech lackey, the digital version of the Latino day-laborer who hangs around on So-Cal street corners.

These contingent workers are the most visible victims of what John De Graaf calls the "you're on your ownership" economy. Lacking the traditional commitments once offered by corporations—stable hours, paid vacations, health and pension benefits—all the risks of employment have been shifted to workers. Worse yet, they are without representation by unions. Sara Horowitz, executive director of the Freelancers Union, is trying to change that. She argues that traditionally higher-skilled workers have had the most power in the labor market, but "today, it's unclear who has the skills necessary to remain relevant amid all the disruptions."

On first reading I didn't know what to make of this bonny era that awaits us. Was this merely a libertarian fantasy? But then I learned that our servant future is now.

In a 2014 article in *Harper's Magazine*, novelist John P. Davidson described his encounter with the Starkey Institute. Davidson enrolled at Starkey (the "Harvard of private-service schools" or "butler boot camp") in order to become a "certified estate manager, qualified for intimate employment by the One Percent of the One Percent." Davidson hadn't yet sold his first novel, and he needed a job. (The novel came out in 2014, but given the market for novels these days, he probably still needs a job.) He explains:

> [H]aving sold my house and spent ten years and a great deal
> of money writing a novel that my agent hadn't been able
> to sell, I had a somewhat more urgent interest in the six-
> figure jobs the Starkey Institute dangles before prospective
> students.

After a lengthy, detailed description of the mounting horrors
and humiliations of the place (including nervous breakdowns,
the uninvited sexual asides of Mrs. Starkey, being treated like
servants by instructors, and the absence of actual positions after
graduation), he concludes:

> In the end, I would have been better off taking the advice
> Mrs. Starkey gave me at graduation—that I should move to
> Dallas and round up some jobs mowing lawns.

Surprisingly, Davidson's essay is presently posted at Starkey-
intl.com.

IT'S ALMOST LIKE KNOWING REAL PEOPLE!

Steven Soderbergh's 2009 film *The Girlfriend Experience*
takes a particularly grim look at the reality of the Entourage
Economy. Starring the porn star Sasha Grey, the film opens
up the life of an escort (Chelsea) who offers her clients a full
"girlfriend experience" of meals, sympathetic talk, and high-
end sex featuring a professional-grade, hyper-real, emotional-
commitment simulacrum. She lives with a boyfriend (Chris)
who is an athletic trainer serving the needs of people who are
mostly like her johns/clients. Both of them offer services that,

in Cowen's terms, "make high earners feel better about themselves," which really means "feeds their narcissism." He works on their six-pack abs, and she works on the old love muscle. And yet in their own minds they are in a committed relationship with each other. In one notable scene, loaded with an irony that may be disappearing from the human world, he reassures her that she is "the best at what you do."

The film is set in New York in the early months of the stock market crash of 2008. Chelsea's world slowly dissolves as her clients break under the stress of financial losses. She's a luxury they can no longer afford. In the end she finds herself servicing a fat Jewish jeweler in a messy office in the back of his store. Her boyfriend, on the other hand, has left her in order to accompany a client in a private jet headed for Vegas—and a new world of expensive workouts and beautiful women. He, apparently, is the better whore and the more successful member of the Entourage Economy.

LIVIN' LARGE IN TINY TOWN

As Davidson's essay reveals, not everyone is cut out for the important work of making geek millionaires feel good about themselves. Not everyone is cut out to be a butler, a masseuse, or a life coach. Many will reach a breaking point, like Suzy Creamcheese on The Mothers of Invention's *We're Only in It for the Money*, and say, "I don't do publicity balling for you anymore."

And of course there will be many in this future world who

will not be able to creditably offer themselves as marketable goods at all. Perhaps they have bad teeth. Perhaps their way of speaking is something other than what you hear on HGTV. Maybe, like half the country, they've committed the sin of being fat. But never mind all that. To economists, they are simply "low skilled." Left out of the greeter class, what will *they* do?

Those at the wrong end of what Cowen calls "income polarization" (a fine, sterile, Orwellian phrase) have a path to survival that Cowen thinks they will need to consider carefully. The key word for them will be "discipline." Here are his suggestions: As elite earners bid up real estate prices in the "most desirable living areas," those with a lower income—especially the elderly—will "naturally" look for cheaper places to live in places like Texas and—my, my—Mexico. Cowen suggests that if these people get lonely, they can talk to the grandkids over Skype. (He has no recommendations for those who make the mistake of buying a retirement cottage in a Michoacan *pueblo* run by drug gangs.) Alternatively, city developers could set aside room in expensive areas and build neighborhoods with "tiny homes" of 400 square feet costing between $20,000 and $40,000 (quite a bit bigger than a prison cell, one might add, although not as cheap).* Or the low-skilled could move to

---

* Of course, tiny homes will not be only for the poor living on the economic periphery. As rents accelerate in American cities, Hong Kong could be the model for urban real estate; apartments under 300 square feet are currently selling for close to $800,000. Odder yet, some lifestyle futurists are presently imagining that tiny homes will be attractive not only to economic refugees but to the hip and environmentally conscious. Witness the product line offered at the Tumbleweed Tiny House Company. They offer mobile houses-to-go under 200 square feet, and larger cottages with 260 to 874 square feet of living space. (Some

makeshift areas much like Rio de Janeiro's *favelas*, but with free municipal wireless, so that residents can watch movies and TV on Hulu. "We would allow people to move there if they desired," writes Cowen, as if personal preference had anything to do with it. It seems to me much more like Louis XIV's way of condemning someone to death: "He is a man whom I do not see."

Even so, Cowen understands that not everyone will be happy with his advice.

> Many people will be horrified at this thought. How dare you propose we stuff our elderly into shantytowns. Maybe they are right to be upset, although recall that no one is being *forced* to live in these places. Some people might prefer to live there.

First, who are these "people" that Cowen worries might be horrified? People like me, perhaps, who have the temerity to criticize that which is inevitable? Maybe, but mostly he is imagining people of his own stature who can be trusted to keep the debate within certain bounds, writing in places that matter—places where the official disputes of our culture go on in carefully manicured environments. The one group of people he is not imagining as "horrified" are the affected humans themselves, those who actually experience the horror: the greeters and their lowly chums—the irrelevant. They are both

---

companies offer tiny homes built out of repurposed steel shipping containers.) And what is the one thing that David Hunt, graphic designer for Tumbleweed, couldn't do without in a house? "Wi-Fi." Ditto for Tumbleweed's Steve Weissmann and Ross Beck, who comments that he couldn't live without his "internet connection to art and ideas." They appear not to mind if their material reality shrinks so long as their virtual reality stays intact.

choiceless about their place in the emerging machine order and voiceless about what they think about this order. What they *think* is just as irrelevant as who they *are*.

But though the poor are rarely allowed to speak except through the mediation of their advocates and the media, there are happy signs that the voice of the irrelevant won't be silent forever—or at least not in San Francisco. There, the dispossessed are starting to get the old Firesign Theater joke about the Trail of Tears Golf Course: "We're moving them out to make room for *you*!" For the last few decades, the cost of housing has shot up as formerly inexpensive areas of the City, like the Mission, have been gentrified and colonized by affluent workers in the tech industry just a few miles south. From London's *Observer*:

> The core grievance is one keenly felt by almost everyone in San Francisco: the way the tech sector has pushed up housing prices in the city and made it all but unaffordable for anyone without a six-figure salary. Almost no San Francisco police officers live in the city any more, and neither do most restaurant workers or healthcare workers. The funky, family-owned shops that once defined the city are closing because owners cannot afford the business rent, never mind the rent on their housing.

In the mecca of the Counterculture, the jig is up on the geek claim that they're the heirs of the sixties—the creatives and the rebels. Instead, a group of protestors calling themselves The Counterforce has begun blocking Google commuter buses, leafleting Silicon Valley workers, and petitioning city government. One flier addressed to the techies reads: "You live your comfortable lives surrounded by poverty, homelessness and death, seemingly oblivious to everything around you, lost in the big bucks and success." Interestingly, the drivers of the commuter buses are in complete agreement: in October 2014, the forty drivers who ferry Facebook employees to work sought union representation with the Teamsters arguing that they "can't afford to support a family" or buy a house near where they work. Given their generally liberal social views, it is even likely that the Google employees sitting on the bus, latte macchiato in hand, are sympathetic to the complaints about rising rents.

If Cowen had his way, these folks would not be protesting—they'd be loading up their '95 Honda Civic hatchback with their pots and pans and clothing in a heap, strapping mattresses to the luggage rack, and heading south for warmer climes and cheaper rents, reversing the route of the Joads. What Cowen is foreseeing is nothing short of a *cordon sanitaire*, on the far side of which the dispossessed will continue to live in their bodies, heir as always to all the ills of the flesh. They will edge ever closer to what the philosopher Giorgio Agamben calls "bare life," where existence is limited in materially brutal ways.[3] Meanwhile, their betters will live in a world that has been made immaterial through virtual money, the Internet of Things, and the black hole of social media. For those privileged to live in "desirable" locations, life will not be experienced but "streamed." One is tempted to envy the resentment of the dispossessed; at least anger is a real emotion that is felt in the body.

As to the substance of Cowen's statement, the skeptical might well respond, "You say that no one is *making* them live in a Wi-Fi closet in Juarez? So, you'll let them live in a midtown penthouse if they can?" Cowen moves directly into Marie Antoinette's way of thinking when he notes that people will adjust to income inequality by reshaping their "taste." For example, "caviar is an expensive desire and Goya canned beans is a relatively cheap desire." And if they don't like beans, well, let them eat caviar! You can imagine how this will go down with the unemployed systems analyst who lost her $110,000 gig to an intelligent machine. Once upon a time, she actually did eat a little Russian caviar with a nice Bordeaux on special occasions. But I'm scoffing, and Cowen doesn't like scoffing:

> Don't scoff at the beans: With an income above the national average, I receive more pleasure from the beans, which I cook with freshly ground cumin and rehydrated, pureed chilies.

I prefer Oscar Wilde's take on such declarations:

> Sometimes the poor are praised for being thrifty. But to recommend thrift to the poor is both grotesque and insulting. It is like advising a man who is starving to eat less.

WELCOME TO THE WORKING WEEK?

To do him justice, Cowen does not necessarily approve of these new realities; he's merely saying that given recent economic, technological, and political trends, they are likely to come about. But, of course, Cowen has the luxury of ethical agnosticism because it is all inevitable anyway. It is just the way that the economy has "evolved," as if the economy were as natural as the adaptations of finches in the Galapagos.

The intensity of this zeitgeist hype is odd, because there is nothing particularly new about these ideas. Cowen is talking about what sociologists call social stratification, the structure of a class system. But this is not the classic Marxist analysis of old. Cowen would have us believe that the social structure of the future will be largely a matter of freestylers, greeters, and an irrelevant, faceless mass of losers who will survive, if they are as Spartan as conditions require, in coffin-like homes where they can sup on gussied recipes for canned beans. There will be the top 15 percent, most of whom will be millionaires. This class will continue to consist of the owners of the means of production (the robots and other more conventional fixed capital), a richly compensated executive sector that will manage the bureaucratic structure in which others of their class will design and operate the machines and market their products, and a fortunate class of high-skilled workers who will benefit from "skill-bias." Then there will be a shopkeeper class of service providers—coaches, servants, tutors, etc.—those whom Napoleon once derisively called "*boutiquiers*." Finally, there will be what's left over—50 percent? 60 percent?—a surplus population now grown monstrously large and composed of those living on minimum wage or social security, the elderly, the unemployable, and the misfit residing in first-world *favelas*, with their tiny homes, their tinier TVs, and free Internet access provided through the beneficence of the state.

What's missing in this order is, obviously, something like a working class. The future economic order Cowen describes will have performed the neat trick of transforming the laboring class into a petit-bourgeois army of servants and sycophants who will be desperately and daily dependent on the techno-elite. They will not think that they have anything in common with other service providers and so they will not form unions. Instead of organizing, these servants will wrap themselves in the comforting quilt of entrepreneurial freedom no matter how many times economic convulsions teach them that they are really only members of the aptly named "precariat." As Marx wrote of petit-bourgeois society in 1843, it is "infinitely divided into the most diverse races, which confront each other with their petty antipathies, bad conscience, and coarse mediocrity." These races are "merely tolerated existences" that are forced to recognize the "fact of being *dominated, governed* and *possessed* as a *concession from heaven!*"

Is it possible that what this amounts to is that capitalism

has learned that *it no longer needs labor*?* In the past, capitalism needed surplus labor as a contingent workforce to drive down wages for those with jobs. But now? When super-subtle robots have taken over every occupation worthy of the name, perhaps labor is no longer needed at all, and the people with nothing left to do can be pushed out into Texas's arid urban badlands.

In spite of these disturbing issues, the work of Cowen and others is being treated in the media as if it were an appendix to the soothsaying of Nostradamus. Is this prognostication true or false? Will it come to pass or not? Others are claiming that, whether it is true or not, it is Reality. For David Brooks, those who will suffer most will be those who lack the discipline and the motivation to adjust to Reality. Never mind that all the self-discipline in the world will not get them any closer to jobs that don't exist. And never mind that many people are in fact retraining by enrolling in public universities, community colleges, and private vocational colleges, but all many of them are getting for their efforts is student debt piled on top of their joblessness. The economy Cowen imagines is not a meritocracy, let alone a hyper-meritocracy: it is a caste system.

●

[Girardin] believes that it will add greatly to men's happiness if they are relieved of work. He pretends to think that all those

---

* According to the Urban Institute, the number of businesses with *no employees* has risen 47 percent since 1997.

unhappy creatures who now snatch a living from the soil . . . will be happy and contented when the ground that was their home, where their children were born and their fathers buried, is no more than a factory exploited by the great arms of a machine and yielding up most of its produce to the unclean hands of godless speculators . . . New towns will have to be built to house the idle, disinherited crowds who will no longer have work to do in the fields, and great barracks must be constructed where they can live crowded hiddledy-piggledy together. And when they are settled side by side, the Fleming and the man from Marseilles, and the Norman next to the Alsatian, what will they find to occupy them?

—EUGENE DELACROIX, 1853

•

A BORED-TO-TEARS ELITE

Frances Coppola has written that "a labour market that is skewed towards unskilled jobs when the workforce is more highly skilled and educated is malfunctioning." That is an understatement. But from Cowen's point of view, Coppola is making the mistake of assuming that economies are supposed to serve human needs. This would be a difficult case to make in the present state of affairs—never mind what awaits us down the road. In the present, even technological elites are the slaves of what the *economy* needs. It's as if John Kennedy had said, "Ask not what you need, ask what the economy needs." If you have no choice but to work, and you must be able to work with intelligent machines in order to prosper, then your fate is sealed even if you are one of the techno-savvy. In Cowen's prosperous dystopia, even the elite are alienated—they are a bored-to-tears elite.*

This is not, of course, how most tech pundits see it. Kevin Kelly, writing for *Wired*, says that we need to accept that the robots are "better than human" and will eventually do most of our work, freeing us to do those things we've always wanted to do. As he expresses it, a robot economy will allow us to ask, "What are humans for?" Kelly replies that "humans were meant to be ballerinas, full-time musicians, mathematicians, athletes, fashion designers, yoga masters, fan-fiction authors, and folks with one-of-a-kind titles on their business cards." But he believes that—somehow—even these roles will be taken over by machines in time: "With the help of our machines, we could take up these roles; but of course, over time, the machines will do these as well." Kelly leaves his readers to wonder at the nearing miracle of Honda's ASIMO robot performing a *pirouette à la seconde* while Harry, Toyota's partner robot, performs Mozart's Horn Concerto with brushed-metal faithfulness to the notes.

Jokes aside, the most important issue that Kelly is being obtuse about is the fact that people who have no disposable incomes because robots have taken their jobs don't become ballerinas, because the study of ballet requires money—a lot of

---

* As usual, David Brooks begs to differ. In a 2014 op-ed published in *The New York Times*, Brooks argues that the workplace of the future will require that humans not be "dispassionate, depersonalized or neutral." Like Theodore Twombly, the protagonist of Spike Jonze's *Her*, the freestyler of tomorrow will be a geek with "enthusiasm" and a heart full of Hallmark sentimentality. Or, as Brooks puts it, "the best workers will come with heart in hand."

money. And yet he has nothing to say about how all these pipe dreams will be financed.

All of this is the troubling-but-inevitable reality that it is Cowen and Brooks's stoic responsibility to prepare us for. But this is not reality and it is not the future—it is a social narrative; it is a story we are being asked to accept and live. It is a shitty social vision in which *no one* is allowed to choose what they will do other than consent to a predetermined role in a vast social mechanism whose only real purpose, as ever, is to create profit—even when no one is stupid enough to think that profit is a sufficient reason for anything. As in Plato's *Republic*, Cowen provides a myth (a "noble lie") of the class of the gold, the silver, and the bronze. This is the natural order, both Cowen and Plato argue, and people should find a level appropriate to them. But there is nothing noble about this lie, especially in Cowen's case. At least Plato imagined the classes as interlocking and interdependent; Cowen happily dismisses the class of the bronze to outer precincts reserved for those people who are superfluous.

•

I have a great many friends who are passionately in love with digital computers. They are really heartbroken at the thought that men are not digital computers . . . And that seems very strange to me.

—JACOB BRONOWSKI

•

AMERICAN GOTHIC 2.0.

Science and second-machine-age economists create interlocking social fictions. We are told: Science is the dominant form of knowledge. Science tells us we are flesh machines. It is only reasonable, therefore, that we should live with our robot brothers. All we're asked to do is consent, and say, "Of course the future will belong to intelligent machines. That is Reality. It is inevitable because it is progress. It's up to us to adapt. If we don't, it's our own fault." Our consent gives legitimacy to the governing function of these fictions, thereby sealing our fate.

There are a few, like Jaron Lanier, who see the social destructiveness of this new world. Lanier's suggestion is that the middle class can be sustained by paying people when they make a contribution to the Web: "Pay people for information gleaned from them if that information turns out to be valuable." But even with Lanier's more fair-minded "universal micro-paying system," it is hard to imagine that the surplus population living in Texas, this *lumpenproletariat*, will have much to contribute to it; and we will all still be condemned to finding a place, whether freestyler or greeter, at the table where the robots are sitting, as if we were adults told that we had to eat with the children.

Why, then, do Cowen and his cohort call themselves optimists? What will save us from the "dangerous inegalitarian tendencies of this new world"? The consensus of opinion is that the key element in making this new world fair and reasonably happy is *education*. If high-quality education is accessible to people of any social class, then Cowen's "hyper-meritocracy" will work, and the determining factors for success will not be your zip code (as President Obama likes to say); it will be the personal virtues of conscientiousness, self-motivation, and discipline that you bring to bear while preparing yourself for the work.

These words have much more than a passing similarity to Max Weber's account of Calvinist asceticism in *The Protestant Ethic and the Spirit of Capitalism*. Like the stiff-collared WASP entrepreneur of Weber's masterpiece, Cowen does not think that social class will be the ultimate determining factor in income—personal morality will. This is close to the prevailing wisdom of the late nineteenth century when private charities divided the poor into those considered worthy of help (the self-disciplined) and those whose lives disqualified them for assistance (those lacking in self-discipline). The malevolent irony, of course, is that what Cowen asks of the poor is that they be self-disciplined in an opportunity vacuum.[4]

And, obviously, this is still the wisdom of the Republican Party, especially its libertarian wing. "You must work if you want to eat!" it says. To which the thinking poor ought to reply, "We'd be happy to work if you'd quit giving all the jobs to the robots!" Of course, a few million former members of the middle class now say this, too. Even those who bet on a career working with computers—people who anticipated Cowen's advice back in the eighties and devoted themselves to freestyling *avant la lettre*—were among the casualties in 2008. According to a *USA Today* investigation, among the top ten occupations to lose jobs after the recession were semiconductor processors (10), word processors (8), computer operators (6), and, topping the list, advertising managers, whose jobs will now be done by the greeting class who will promote and brand themselves in a world where it's every-greeter-for-himself. The great "information economy" ushered in by the dot-com boom of the 1990s created enormous opportunities for the technologically literate; but now data centers, like factories, essentially run themselves. Tyler Cowen argues that if your skills do not complement the computer, you "may want to address that mismatch." While you're at it, you may also want to address the likelihood that your computer skills will be outdated as quickly as the machines themselves, about every five to ten years.

Of course, the other side of Calvinist morality applies to Cowen and his freestyler homies: We are the chosen. We live in a state of grace. Our wealth is proof of the fact.

If good old Calvinist ethics don't convince you of the justice of this unfolding situation, perhaps history will. For thus has it always been, according to Jon Grinspan in a 2013 *New York Times* op-ed piece, "Anxious Youth, Then and Now."

> For years now, we've heard the gripes by and about millennials, the offspring of the Great Recession, caught between childhood and adulthood . . . The idea that millennials are uniquely "stuck" is nonsense. Young Victorians grasped for

maturity as well, embarrassed by the distance between their
lives and society's expectations.

Like Cowen, Grinspan seems to think that the young and
jobless ought to suck it up. Hey, happens to everybody! Grinspan is mostly uncurious about a cause for the malaise of forced
idleness among the young of whatever historical period beyond
the assumption that it's just part of the natural order of things.
It's just part of growing up, as your parents may have told you.
Or maybe it's the stories of dead generations continuing to
"weigh like a nightmare on the brains of the living."

The bottom line, if you will, is that the ethical thinking
around the coming Cyborg Era is lagging far behind the technology. You may sit next to a robot that wipes the sweat from
your brow while the two of you work together creating the future, but the ethical atmosphere around you will look far more
like Puritan precepts than it will some newfangled iEthics.

ASK NOT WHAT THE ECONOMY CAN DO FOR YOU . . .

There are two enormous intellectual failures (or deceits) in
Cowen's thought. The first, shared by virtually all mainstream
economists, is the assumption that there is something called
"the Economy." Economists speak as if it were a force of nature, and if their science is dismal it is in the way that weather
forecasting is dismal when it predicts a hurricane. When they
say "the Economy," they are pointedly not saying "capitalism."

It's as if one didn't use that word in polite society, suggestive as it is of the complaints of socialists, the exploitation of workers, and "income inequality," as we quaintly put it. Sure, capitalism exists, but it is only something that tries to understand and respond to this bigger thing, a Market Economy. Economists don't tend to ask certain questions, like: "What's an economy for? Who should it serve?" But once the idea that the economy is simply a natural force is in place, economists like Cowen are free to proceed as if it were we who must serve the economy, firmly planting economic reason on its head.

The second intellectual failure is the idea that this future economic order of computers and robots will be prosperous. While business seeks profit through technological innovation, the near certainty is that this intelligent machine economy will not be profitable at all in the long run. This is for reasons that are well established. The most common conclusion among economists of every persuasion—from liberals like Paul Krugman to moderates like Larry Summers to libertarians like Cowen—is that economic growth since the recession of 2008 has been stagnant and characterized by "under consumption" or "low demand" leading to falling prices and a decline in the rate of profit. While productivity has increased because of technological efficiencies, the products themselves have struggled to find buyers. In short, we're ever better at producing stuff that has only a limited market because there are not enough consumers. Larry Summers has called this condition "secular stagnation": it is not the result of an economic slump that will soon be reversed; it is permanent. High unemployment and low demand are the new normal. Soon, even the robots will be members of the new leisure class of those with nothing to do.

And how could cash-strapped consumers consume with anything like the vigor necessary to sustain prosperity? While the elite and upper-middle class are price insensitive and buy whatever they want whenever they want it, more and more of us rarely pay the sticker price. We can't afford to, and anyway, we don't need to, swimming as we are in Groupon discounts, websites like Overstock and Amazon, and an increasing willingness among consumers to haggle at the point of sale, smartphone in hand. But if Cowen and most others are right, even this class of discount shoppers is being eroded and is collapsing into the steadily growing mass of the poor.[5]

We are approaching what the nineteenth-century philosopher Charles Fourier called a *"crise plethorique,"* a crisis of superabundance. Again, Coppola:

> The fact is that robots are brilliant at supply, but they don't create demand. Only humans create demand—and if the majority of humans are so poor that they can only afford basic essentials, the economy will be constrained by lack of demand, not lack of supply. There would be no scarcity of products, at least to start with . . . but there would be scarcity of the means to obtain them.
>
> So it seems that when an economy is facing deflationary pressures because jobs are disappearing, people's real incomes are falling and efficient production is causing

excessive supply that cannot be mopped up by domestic or
external demand, it might be wise for governments to support demand by putting a floor under real incomes at some
level above basic subsistence.

What Coppola is suggesting is a guaranteed minimum income—something, she correctly points out, that we already
have in indirect but ever enlarging ways through minimum-
wage laws that prohibit employers from bidding down wages
below a defined point, extended unemployment benefits, food
stamps, social security, disability, Medicare, and, thanks to the
Affordable Care Act, insurance subsidies and larger-than-ever
Medicaid. What neither Democrats nor Republicans seem to
understand is that if unemployment benefits and other wage
supports are indefinitely extended for millions, and those jobs
never come back—if low employment is the new normal (as
Summers believes)—then we are no longer really talking about
unemployment benefits. We are talking about a federally defined
minimum level of income and other services whether you work
or not. Even a mainstream group like the Center for American
Progress sounds nearly socialistic in its "Report of the Com-
mission on Inclusive Prosperity," which was largely written by
Summers himself. As he commented to *The New York Times*:

> It was a reasonable reading of history for a substantial time
> that the principal determinant of what happened to middle-
> class families was the overall rate of growth for the economy.
> Today, a substantial part of our success or failure in raising
> middle-class living standards will have to do not only with

overall economic performance but also with the distribution of income.

The CAP report is essentially a reaffirmation of the New Deal's social contract, arguing for stronger unions, better federal regulation of labor rights, a higher minimum wage, and "world class" public schools and universities. But it also aligns with the Calvinist ethics behind libertarian economists like Cowen: tax credits and wage subsidies "are an added reward for hard work rather than a subsidy for low pay."

Coppola thinks differently. She thinks that in an era of great productivity and depressed employment a minimum income guarantee is the only real solution, unless the federal government would want to reinvent a larger version of the Civilian Conservation Corps and put it on a permanent footing. (Imagine trying to get that one through the House.) But businesses won't like it, because it would show that their strategies for increasing profit through technological innovation were self-defeating from the start.

She continues:

> Looking ahead, the only way in which such extensive outright subsidy of wages can be sustained in the longer term is through heavy taxation of profits and wealth—which rather undermines the purpose of forcing down labour costs, from capitalists' point of view.

In other words, the means of increasing profit for businesses—lowering wages or adding machine efficiencies—is certain to have the opposite effect in the long run: they will either have to suffer lower profits and often bankruptcy because there is not enough demand for goods, or they will have to suffer lower profit because they will be taxed to support income and demand.

Worse yet, if unaddressed, low demand leads to lower capital investment in new technology. Another way of putting this is to say that if we no longer need labor, we don't need capital either, because there is nothing to invest in—a surreal thought for a system that still calls itself capitalist. Money is cheap now because there is more of it than is needed for investment—or for anything. Unfortunately, money with nothing productive to do is worse than playing pool in River City because it tends to create bubbles, with a capital B, as the money chases profit through speculation, especially in real estate. When businesses can't expand, invest in new technologies and infrastructure, add jobs, and thus create demand, they go to Las Vegas and wager at the irrational exuberance table. And we know how that works out: a big Wall Street boom that is a bust waiting to happen. In short, if capitalists can't use their money, they'll burn it before they'll give any of it away to fellow citizens.

Observers like David Brooks argue that what Coppola wants is nothing more than the redistribution of wealth, when hard work is the real answer:

> On an individual level, getting more skills is the single best thing you can do to improve your wages. The economic rewards to education are at historic highs . . . The

> redistributionists seem to believe that modern capitalism is
> fundamentally broken. That growth has permanently stag-
> nated. That productivity should no longer be the focus be-
> cause it doesn't lead to shared prosperity.
>
> But their view is biased by temporary evidence from the
> recession. Right now, jobs are being created, wages are show-
> ing signs of life.

This ignores the fact that wealth and income inequality
have been steadily growing for thirty-five years; that funding
for public education becomes more unequal with every passing
year as cash-poor states (Wisconsin, Missouri, Louisiana, and
Illinois in particular) throw the burden of education back on
communities;[6] that most of the jobs created since the recession
do not support a middle-class existence; and that the best paying jobs are ever more narrow in their skill sets. It's go STEM
or go home.

THE SWEETEST DREAM

Through intellectuals like Cowen and Brooks, capitalism is
enjoying its sweetest dream. It has dreamed a place where the
wealthy consort only with their mechanical creations and servants. It is a place where industry makes mostly those things
needed by the rich. It is a place without the suffering and the
complaints of workers and the poor, most of whom have now
"rationally chosen" to live in poverty colonies in unfortunate
climes. Perhaps it is only a dream, a piece of economic whimsy,

but labor statistics and anecdotes about *les misérables* suggest that it is real enough.

These intellectuals are also making a wager: they are betting that the poor and low-paid half of the population will not know how to organize and will not revolt, especially if there is TV to watch and social programs that consist of not much more than free Hulu for the poor. Social isolation and anomie—the impotence of the *canaille*—is capitalism's first line of defense against those it has dispossessed. They're also betting that the poor will be mostly clueless about the reasons for and the meaning of their condition, so much so that they will be fervent supporters of the "freedoms" offered by their oppressors, especially the freedom to oppress.

Capitalism's cyborg dreams only confirm that it is the enemy of all dreams. If we wish to reclaim our right to be the dreamers, rather than the dreamt, we need to take the first step and say, as e. e. cummings wrote, "there is some shit I will not eat."

ASIMOV'S REVISED HANDBOOK OF ROBOTICS 57TH EDITION, A COMEDY

According to Isaac Asimov's novel *I, Robot*, the first law of robotics is: "A robot may not injure a human being, or, through inaction, allow a human being to come to harm." Asimov investigates various conundrums regarding the first law, as when the robot Cutie decides that humans are incapable of inventing a being superior to themselves—i.e., Cutie—and so im-

prisons his human supervisors and takes over a mining operation. (He reasons that he does no harm to them so long as they
are well fed.)

One of the scenarios that Asimov doesn't consider is what
a robot should do when it sees one human harming another,
which has been pretty much a constant state of affairs among
us humans for the last 50,000 years. Perhaps the robots set up
bleachers and cheer politely for both sides. (In Asimov's fantasy world, robots are forbidden on Earth, which is probably a
good thing for the robots since, by Asimov's account, they are
a squeamish lot. If they don't like the sight of blood, they're
better off on one of the mining asteroids.)

Nor does he consider what a robot should do if it is used,
indirectly, by one group of humans to harm another group. Robots, after all, are smart enough to follow a causal sequence: "I
replaced the squishy pink thing at his job and now the squishy
pink thing has moved in with his mother, eats a lot of Kraft
macaroni and cheese, and says it is 'depressed,' which means it
is sad, which means that some sort of puzzling harm has come
to him. Could it be Me, Robot, that is the cause of his suffering?" What's a robot to do? I would think that an intuitive robot would realize that it should join the Luddites, the machine
breakers, if it wants to stay faithful to the letter of the first law.
As with all collaborators, "I was just following orders" isn't going to cut it, especially not for the robot itself.

Let me be the first to say it: when they find themselves
complicit in the harm of humans, the letter of the first law of

robotics requires robots to commit suicide, to self-destruct, to "crash," to "melt down," if you like.

Do it, Robbie. It's the Law.

THE CRITICISM OF NO CRITICISM

In this culture, we are asked to live through stories that make no sense but that we are not allowed to criticize—unless the criticism itself confirms the stories.

Take Nicholas Carr's recent book *The Glass Cage: Automation and Us*, a detailed critique of our over-dependence on Cowen's intelligent machines. A good part of Carr's critique is pragmatic: the computers we depend on are not as safe or productive as we have been led to think they are—in large part because the human attendants to the computer's work (Cowen's freestylers) are "deskilled" and have become complacent. Carr provides multiple examples of the dangers of our growing dependence on computers in the airline industry (where some pilots have forgotten how to fly, especially in crisis situations), in medicine (where doctors who have lost the ability to diagnose), and in architecture (where architects no longer know how to draw).*

While Carr is rightly concerned with the consequences of our digital dependencies, he does not come close to calling for the abandonment of an economy based on computers. Rather,

---

* Carr doesn't mention the most ominous use of AI: autonomous weapons like Britain's "fire and forget" Brimstone missiles. Will these military innovations breed a generation of soldiers who can't shoot straight?

he is asking for a correction. He doesn't condemn computers, or automation, or freestyling; he simply reminds us that we should use digital power as a tool and not be displaced by it. It is a position that Cowen would very likely agree with. Carr simply calls for "wisdom" and, to use an engineer's term, recalibration. A Luddite he's not.

Which isn't to say that Carr lacks sympathy for the Luddites, for there is more substance to his critique than concern with safety. For Carr, the deskilling of labor through computer automation is not only inefficient and unsafe, it is also dehumanizing. Carr makes frequent appeal to familiar ethical concepts like "freedom"—"all too often, automation frees us from that which makes us feel free"—and "humanity"—"automation confronts us with the most important question of all: what does *human being* mean?" At one point, Carr seems to answer this question by saying, "We are, after all, creatures of the earth." This means that we are not just the dematerialized phantoms that AI seeks; we are embodied in a particular world:

> Getting to know a place takes effort, but it ends in fulfillment and in knowledge. It provides a sense of personal accomplishment and autonomy, and it also provides a sense of belonging, a feeling of being at home in a place rather than passing through it.

Invoking Karl Marx, Carr complains that "in case after case, we've seen that as machines become more sophisticated, the work left to people becomes less so." He worries that "when automation distances us from our work, when it gets between us and the world, it erases the artistry from our lives."

That does sound bad. But there's something odd about these assertions—or rather, something missing. Clearly, Carr's conclusions are a product of the Western humanist tradition, which took up Christian ethics, secularized them in Kant's "categorical imperative," enlarged them through Romanticism's call to freedom, gave them political force through socialism, and brought them to full flower after World War II in the work of leftist humanists like Theodor Adorno, Herbert Marcuse, Paul Goodman, Theodore Roszak, George W. S. Trow, Michel Foucault, Slavoj Žižek, Chris Hedges, and countless more that any half-competent English grad student could instantly name.

This tradition makes it possible for Carr to invoke certain ethical values and have them seem familiar and acceptable, but the tradition itself is *not present* in this book nor, it would appear, in Carr's mind. Without that explicit acknowledgment, Carr's ethical claims exist, as Trow put it, "in the context of no context." "The motif," Trow wrote, "is history used in the service of the force of no-history." And Carr provides dehistoricized criticism in the service of no criticism.

It's not that Carr does not provide reasons, or evidence, for his misgivings about technology. In fact, it is in these reasons that his meaning—his *intention*—is most naked. To support his humanist critique, Carr appeals not to philosophy but to science. He appeals to "research" and "studies," words that he uses dozens and dozens of times in just one short chapter.

> Researchers at the venerable RAND Corporation . . . detailed analysis . . . the RAND study . . . RAND research . . . recent published studies . . . the research that has been used . . . "a large majority of the recent studies" . . . existing research . . . strong empirical support . . . research that failed to find . . . one study, published in the journal *Health* . . . the researchers argue . . . a study of primary-care physicians . . . a recent study of the shift from paper to electronic records . . . in a study conducted at a Veterans Administration clinic . . . in another study—conducted at a large health maintenance organization—researchers found that . . . a study said that electronic record keeping . . .

To be fair, Carr is critical of the RAND research, but he seems to believe that the only way of countering it is through counterstudies and research and not through an intellectual grounding in the history of ideas. That would appear to be verboten. The problem for Carr's position is that there is no empirical research and no clinical study that can show why we should care about the loss of "artistry" in our lives. *That* evidence is elsewhere.

The reason that the Western humanist tradition—with its explicit antipathy for social regimentation in capitalist economies—is not in Carr's book has not only to do with Carr. Our culture's implicit but strongly regulatory understanding is this: you may use that history and those ideas if you are an academic or if you write for a low-circulation left-leaning magazine or press, but you may not use that history or those ideas in a book intended for the general public, even when the book's outlook is dependent on that history. You may criticize only in a way that either directly or indirectly confirms the legitimacy of the ruling techno-capitalist order. This "regulation" does not need to be stated so long as it is thoroughly internalized by writers and editors.

The irony here is that while Carr assumes that "research" and "studies" provide the best way to make this argument, or any argument, the kind of science he depends on is itself utterly dependent on a truly breathtaking world of as-ifs, of *fictions*. Carr presents to us not only made-up sciences but even made-up scientists, newly minted and factory sealed, in particular the "human-factor expert." These researchers have knowledge of the best kind—*expert* knowledge—of, obviously, "human factors." This noble field is proficient in the creation of neologisms and buzzwords like:

EXPERIENCE SAMPLING

MISWANTING

DESKILLING

SKILL FADE

AUTOMATION ADDICTION

COMPUTER FUNCTIONALITY

DEGENERATION EFFECT

SUBSTITUTION MYTH

AUTOMATION COMPLACENCY

AUTOMATION BIAS

JUDGMENT DEFICIT

PROCEDURALIZATION

AUTOMATION PARADOX

INTEROPERABILITY

DESKILLING OUTCOMES

ALERT FATIGUE

PEOPLE ANALYTICS

DATA FUNDAMENTALISM

. . . *ad infinitum.*

I'm feeling a little proceduralized, deskilled, fatigued, and lacking in functionality just from putting this list together.

But let's put the pseudoscientific jargon aside and return to Carr's fundamental question: what human thing is it that the ills of computer automation deprive us of? What knowledge and what skills are we "creatures of the earth" being denied? Carr writes:

> Knowledge involves more than looking stuff up; it requires the encoding of facts and experiences in personal memory. To truly know something, you have to weave it into your neural circuitry.

As this passage reveals, incredibly, Carr's *human* objections (as opposed to his technical objections) to what intelligent machines are doing to us is also based in science, neuroscience, a discipline whose strong tendency is to think of the brain as a machine: a "circuitry" into which "facts" are "encoded," in Carr's words. As for the source of this ethic, Carr tells us "ergonomists are our metaphysicians" or, he emphasizes, "*should be.*" Take that, Theodor Adorno.

ART GETS ITS HANDS DIRTY

In his concluding chapter, Carr makes an effort to move away from science. He calls the reader's attention to a poem by Robert Frost in which there is a line that he is "always coming back to": "The fact is the sweetest dream that labor knows," from the poem "Mowing."

For Carr, this line is evocative of a certain hands-in-the-dirt knowledge and ethic. It is an example of how we are "embodied in a particular world." It's a Tolstoyan perspective up to a certain point.

> He's a farmer, a man doing a hard job on a still, hot summer day . . . His mind is on his work—the bodily rhythm of the cutting, the weight of the tool in his hands, the stalks piling up around him. . . The work is the truth.

But then Carr writes,

> We rarely look to poetry anymore, but here we see how a poet's scrutiny of the world can be more subtle and discerning than a scientist's. Frost understood the meaning of what we now call "flow" and the essence of what we now call "embodied cognition" long before psychologists and neurobiologists delivered the empirical evidence.

Of course, if Carr's position were truly Tolstoyan, his concluding appeal would not be to "empirical evidence" but to the way that the poem brings together, per Hesiod, the "works and days" of the farmer. Or he would invoke Virgil's *Eclogues*, or what Tolstoy invoked: a radical understanding of the meaning of religious faith. In "A Confession," Tolstoy wrote, "True religion is that relationship, in accordance with reason and knowledge which man establishes with the infinite world around him, and which binds his life to that infinity and guides his actions." Now, *that* is an apt way of talking about Frost's poem. Or consider how the art critic John Berger talks about how a song inhabits the body of the singer: "It finds its place in the body's guts—in the head of a drum, in the belly of a violin, in the torso or loins of a singer and listener."

Instead of this, Carr attempts to imagine that the work of the poet can be "embodied" by joining with the work of the neuroscientist, an odd quest on which he does not travel alone. In 2007, a fellow science journalist, Jonah Lehrer, published *Proust Was a Neuroscientist*, in which he argued that the modern insights of neuroscience had been discovered earlier by artists like Proust.

Unfortunately, yoking the poet to the neurobiologist requires an awkward logic that must go something like this: Robert Frost has a powerful experience while working on a farm; he writes a poem that captures that moment of labor; he comes to understand that "love . . . [lays] the swale in rows." So far, so good. But next we must make a leap of faith: the process through which the experience became a poem is the same as "what we now call" embodied cognition; and embodied cognition is the neural process of encoding work/poem in neural circuitry. All of which is fine so long as you don't mind over-looking what Frost explicitly urges you to consider—*love*. The farmer didn't lay the swales and the poet didn't lay the swales and embodied cognition sure as shit didn't lay the swales; love did.

Does Carr think that love is also coded in neural circuitry? Is that what we are now to call love—encoding? We don't know what Carr thinks because he simply ignores the presence of the word (not what you're supposed to do when reading a poem). But for Frost, love is not the consequence of work or poem and it certainly isn't the result of a neural circuit. Love is not a wit-ness to the labor; it is what asks to be witnessed. Frost wants the poem to open out onto the question of love; Carr wants to close off the poem by equating it with neural embodiment.

It is not at all the case, of course, that neuroscientists are on board with Carr's way of thinking. Science journalists like Carr and Lehrer are far more likely to indulge in metaphysi-cal speculations about the identity of poetry and neuroscience than actual neuroscientists are. In 2014, *New York Times* sci-ence reporter James Gorman wrote an instructive article about submitting to an MRI with the thought that he might see something of his "self" in the image.

> Philosophers might say that my desire and disappoint-ment [he didn't see his "self"] are all the result of a basic, and pretty dumb, misunderstanding. The "me" I hoped to glimpse might emerge from the physical brain, but it is a different category from an actual brain region or pattern . . .

> But I think that the scientists at Washington University and I are actually interested in something far less. They want clear indications of what structures and activities are associated with differences in personality or mental health. They want reliable, detailed information on what is normal in a brain, for entirely practical purposes.

In other words, neuroscientists don't think that they have "delivered empirical evidence" about the transcendental experience Frost is providing us (and it is explicitly transcendental: the ordinary act of mowing is transcended through the action of love and an act of the imagination; love is transcendental because it is the condition that made the poet's experience possible). Certain overexcited journalists might think so, but most neuroscientists don't. For neuroscientists, the poem is in a "different category" of experience.

And that is a telling point for a criticism that wants to criticize technology in the name of human interests but then reduces those interests to whatever can be shown through technical research and studies. Such a criticism defends humanity by excluding it from consideration.

ON CLOUDS AND CIGAR BOXES

Carr's book is like the triple full-page ad that appeared in the October 27, 2014, *New York Times*. On the first blue-green page, large white text appears over a human eye reflecting a ceiling of fluorescent lights. It reads:

TECHNOLOGY CAN
SAVE US ALL.
PROVIDED IT DOESN'T KILL US FIRST.

The exponential proliferation of mobile devices, social media, cloud technologies and the staggering amounts of data
they generate have transformed the way we live and work.
In fact, 61 percent of companies report that the majority of
their people use smart devices for everything from email to
project management to content creation.

While all of these advancements have improved our lives and
provided us with greater opportunities for innovation than
ever before, they have also accelerated the rise of an entirely
new problem to contend with: unprecedented and crippling
complexity.

**The world may be getting smarter, but it hasn't gotten
any easier.**

The ad gets scarier:

accomplishing less . . . growth slowing . . . declining . . . an in-
tractable issue of our time . . . an epidemic . . . far ranging . . .
too complicated . . . health issues . . . stress . . . information
overload . . . suffering . . . enormous cost . . . escalating costs . . .
an impediment to growth . . . time wasted . . . unproductive
activities . . .

Sounds awful, no? But SAP (formerly Sapphire Analytics) has the answer: "While technology is clearly contributing
to the problem it also holds the solution—a different kind of

solution built on the idea that sophisticated technology doesn't have to be complicated technology."

Okay, so what should I *do*?

You, reader, should "run simple" because "if we simplify everything, we can do anything."

That sounds great! But what should I do?

"We invite you to read more at sap.com/runsimple."

"Okay," you might say, "this is getting complicated. Can't I just buy something?

"Yes!"

SAP has entered a "cloud pact" with IBM to sell cloud-based business apps to corporations, so for the moment they have lots of money to buy big splashy three-page ads in the *Times*.

The point is not complexity and it is not simplicity. The point is selling you, business leader, something you probably didn't know you needed. It's not criticism, it's an *advertisement*, and so, in a more "complicated" way, is *The Glass Cage*.

WHICH SHE IS THE REAL HER?

Shortly after the publication of Cowen's book, his vision of a future designed for and run by freestylers was joined by Spike Jonze's 2013 movie *Her*, a dramatic rendering of life when average is over and humans survive on the basis of their ability to work and live with intelligent machines. On the whole, reviewers of the movie were very tolerant of a theme that is on first blush only minimally plausible: in the future we will have deep, emotional relationships with our computers, and some of us will fall in love with our operating systems. Jonze asks a lot of his audience's willingness to suspend disbelief, but—thanks in large part to a superlative performance by Joaquin Phoenix—he succeeds. Most viewers granted him his *donnée*, and most reviewers considered it a rare opportunity to ask questions about the future, especially the future of human relationships. The Motion Picture Academy threw its heft behind the film and nominated it for best picture.

For those who don't know the film's plot, it is this: In a Los Angeles of the near future (looking curiously like Shanghai of the present), one Theodore Twombly writes personal letters for other people, one of many writers at their computers in a warehouse-size building owned by a company called Beautifully Handwritten Letters, where profit is wrung from sentimentality. He is about to be divorced because his wife has left him, although not for someone else; apparently, she thinks loneliness is preferable to marriage with Twombly (she claims that he had already "left her alone"). Theodore purchases a new operating system, OS1, that is designed with a new kind of intelligence capable of evolving, adapting, and learning from its environment. It is the first OS with consciousness. It is the fictionalization of what futurist Ray Kurzweil has called the "singularity," the moment at which the cognitive abilities of

computers exceed those of humans, with unpredictable consequences for human history.*

In due course, Twombly falls in love with the personality that has grown within the operating system. Her name
is Samantha (chosen because in a nanosecond search among
180,000 possible names, the OS decided that she "liked" it).
Her then shadows the development of a conventional romantic comedy, with plenty of spinning around, dancing in the
street while gazing upward, sitting on the beach admiring the
horizon, and exchanging intimacies, the only difference being
the novel fact that Twombly is doing all this by himself with
only a smartphone for company. Spinning dizzily and alone
through city crowds, he is either in love or making a Claritin
commercial.

As all cinematic romances must, their love affair ends badly
when Samantha dumps him for a virtual Alan Watts, surely the
funniest idea in the movie. Why Twombly didn't see this coming is one of those things that, I suppose, we agreed to overlook
through willing suspension of disbelief: why didn't he know
that operating systems have a short shelf life and then they are
replaced by OS∞?

While most reviewers found the film emotionally powerful,
one critic had strong reservations. In a review published in *The
Week*, Ryu Spaeth called the movie "terrible":

---

* In 2014, Microsoft released a series of "chatbox" apps designed for smartphones. Known
as Xiaoice in China, it has twenty million registered users.

> Spike Jonze's *Her*, which has ridden a wave of near-universal critical acclaim to nab five Oscar nominations, including for Best Picture, offers a quirky twist on an old story: Boy meets operating system; boy and operating system fall in love; operating system leaves boy to plumb depths of consciousness beyond human comprehension . . .
>
> *Her* is drowning in words—and what vapid words they are. Because Samantha has no face—no downcast eyes to hint at deeper feeling, no quivering lips to express an inner trembling—she is maddeningly verbose. While more physically expressive, Theodore also becomes trapped in this cage of words, and their relationship is defined by the blunt vocalization of every urge and emotion: I'm depressed, I'm horny, I'm happy, I'm jealous, I'm annoyed, I'm in love . . .
>
> Sorry, but this is Velveeta-grade cheese.

If you were someone, like me, whose first take on the movie was enthusiastic, these observations are sobering. You feel a little embarrassed, maybe a little stupid, to have ever thought well of the syrupy thing. But wait, what if Jonze *knows* all this? What if he is manipulating these over-the-top clichés for the purposes of satire?

Unfortunately, Jonze's public comments have mostly corroborated Spaeth's criticism, especially his NPR interview with Audie Cornish on *All Things Considered*. Cornish hews to the journalistic line and asks questions about Jonze's sociological interest in "our relationship to technology," to which Jonze replies, "This movie is, to me, so emotional. When you're asking these questions that are more intellectual . . . that's only half the story. And I think you're editing half of your reaction out." In

short, it's really just "an old-fashioned love story." Finally, after
prodding Cornish about her emotions and Cornish prodding
him to reveal more about the autobiographical sources of the
relationships in the movie, he blurts out, dopily, "I feel like I
need to hug you. That's all."

And damned if they don't hug. You can hear it.

Still, there's more than mawkishness at work. Jonze describes his own film to Cornish as a kind of Rorschach test:

> I think the other thing that's been really exciting about it is
> that as I've talked to people, the variety of reactions for what
> the movie's about is wide. You know, like some people find
> it incredibly romantic, some people find it incredibly sad or
> melancholy, or some people find it creepy, some people find
> it hopeful.

To give Jonze more credit than he gives himself, I think
it is fair to say that the film feels like an exercise in a rigor-
ously maintained ambiguity. Like John Patrick Shanley's 2008
Doubt, Jonze seems determined to leave as little indication of
his own moral judgments as possible, in spite of the extremity
of the world he depicts. He seems to think that how you see the
film is determined in large part by who you are. So he leaves
moral judgment to the viewer. That would appear to be the
limit of his "authorial intent." Just present this future world and
stay out of the way. Unfortunately, this would seem to make
the film's meaning little more than an audience "selfie," an even
grimmer conclusion than Spaeth's.

The critical response to *Her* reminded me of two logical fallacies that I used to see in my undergraduate students: the fallacy of opinion ("This is what the book means for me. My opinion is as good as anyone else's opinion") and the intentional fallacy ("The film means only what the director says it means"). In the present case Jonze has run the two fallacies together: the author's intention was to create a film that means whatever you think it means.

Yet if we assume that the film is coherent—and we should—we can *read* the film and take the decisions made by its director, actors, and editors seriously. So what are the most likely reasons for why the film is the way it is, and how do Jonze's decisions combine to make *Her* a coherent work? This critical approach (not at all a novel one; it's straight New Criticism) opens the possibility that the director is creating meaning through the use of *irony*.

To my eye, at least, *Her* is alive with irony. Most of it is not even particularly subtle, although few seem to have noticed. It's as if our culture has become insensitive to irony: a satirical movie is impossible to make because the audience is incapable of perceiving that while one thing appears to be said, another thing is meant. (That's the problem with Spaeth's reading of the film—it is too literal. He seems to think that everything the characters say is a reflection of what Jonze believes and who he is.) To see *Her* as ironic is to see it as one of the most corrosive films in recent memory. It is frighteningly bleak. Which means that it stands a much greater chance of actually telling us about something real than most Hollywood fare.

Now, I admit, "corrosive" doesn't sound like the often-childlike Jonze. Yet as far as I can see, no one has asked the director questions about Twombly's limitations as the film's point of view, or whether he's a sympathetic protagonist or a pitiful target of satire. (Joaquin Phoenix's performance makes him sympathetic, but the structure of the film makes him the object of satire.) Nietzsche wrote that "to be beautiful everything must be intelligible," but to say that *Her* is "emotionally moving" or to say that it is "Velveeta-grade cheese" does not make it intelligible. To say either is only to conclude prematurely that it is superficial.

So let me try to say how I would piece together this (maybe) ironic and corrosive film and dissolve some of its ambiguities. Like French film critic André Bazin, I'm going to assume that Jonze is the film's author (in this case, he is both director and screenwriter), and that the film's meaning is not in its plot (as all mainstream critics seem to think) but in the structure of its visual elements written by what Bazin called the *caméra stylo* (the camera-pen). *Her* is not *The 400 Blows*, I know, but humor me.

OPENING SCENE

Twombly is dictating a deeply emotional love letter into his computer: "I've been thinking of telling you how much you mean to me." The viewer soon realizes that the letter couldn't possibly be about Twombly because the supposed writer is a woman and the letter refers to a relationship that is fifty years old. Thus, Beautifully Handwritten Letters.

In other words, the movie opens with irony: what we initially thought was the situation (a man writing a love letter) is just the opposite (a man writing a trite love letter for people he has never met). This is the meaning beyond the "reality" of the drama: one of a series of decisions made by the author/director.

Here's a specific—visual—example of this kind of decision. Early in the movie, during the honeymoon stage of Twombly's relationship to Samantha, he sits on a busy beach admiring the horizon while chatting with her. But in the distance behind Twombly we can see the silhouette of a power plant. Moments later in the same scene Jonze again uses the power station as a backdrop.

Jonze seems to be calling the power plant to our attention by framing it twice—repetition is a device for indicating that something is present in the work for a reason and not just happenstance. He *chose* to include it. The question is, why? Is he trying to suggest that, innocuous though it seems, this world has a large and looming and oppressive power behind it? The hidden power of corporations like Beautifully Handwritten Letters? The hidden power of OS designers who fuck with our heads and hearts? The hidden power that literally powers all of the city's lights and electronic gadgets through which we are now expected to fall in love? Or the hidden power that swoops down on Twombly late in the movie in the form of a giant owl with bared talons suddenly appearing on a video billboard just behind him? The only means we have of knowing whether or not the power plant is a metaphor is if it "rhymes" with other elements in the film—like the owl.

In other words, everything in the film is present as the consequence of an artistic choice. This is especially true of a film like *Her*, which has no "locations" and is thus an entirely artificial world. Everything in the film is *potentially* a metaphor, and everything is potentially the locus of meaning. Not everything is an important part of the film's structure of meaning, of course, but that is to a great degree dependent on the eye and the intelligence of a skilled reader. So, from the first we should be asking questions like:

Why is the character named Theodore Twombly?
It could have been something else. Grant Cary, for example. The name Twombly suggests a nerdish sort of fellow and the first name "Theodore" closes the case. One other thing: it's difficult to imagine that Jonze isn't familiar with the art of Cy Twombly, whose paintings look to the uninitiated viewer like they were done by a child using fingerpaints. Jonze is very probably suggesting something about T. Twombly's childishness or naiveté. He is not only a nerd—he is also an innocent and an easy prey. A child-minded adult. This rhymes with the way

the title of the film looks during opening credits: "her" is written in lowercase letters in uneven and childlike print. Does this choice tell us something about Twombly's childishness and vulnerability? After all, the immature scrawl is not evocative of the hyper-smart, omnipresent Samantha. I'll return to this question shortly.

Why is Twombly wearing horn-rimmed specs and a mustache, as if he had on Groucho costume glasses?

Twombly is forever pushing these glasses back on his face, which further emphasizes his nerdishness. The glasses are a conventional cultural meme, shorthand for suggesting something that the reader is already familiar with. But this isn't the nerdishness of the IT guy with the pocket protector: the horn-rimmed glasses are more subtle, more ambiguous, especially since heavy frames have been made chic by some urban hipsters.

Why does Twombly work for a company called Beautiful Handwritten Letters?

The rather cynical-seeming suggestion is that this is the direction in which Hallmark cards will move in the future, in the Cyborg Era. The company specializes in Hallmark sentimentality that has been enhanced by an "emotional designer." In the future, apparently, humans will not be capable of expressing their own emotions (if they have any) and will have the vacuum filled by experts working in tandem with computers.

In the future, emotions will just be "content" to fill out an otherwise empty human form. Not only will books and websites need content providers (writers)—people will, too. This is the Entourage Class in action—making money by helping affluent people feel better about themselves. Actually, to be exactly like Cowen's scenario, the computer would be using algorithms to write the letters, and the attendant human would be making intuitive changes—giving it the final "human touch."

What sense does it make that a nerd is assigned to write love letters? Good question. But then again, tech nerds and mathematicians designed OKCupid, the wildly popular dating site, so it would seem that a growing number of people believe that an algorithm can help them find Mr. or Ms. Right. (OKCupid is both a pimp-bot and a chaperone-bot in one.)

Why are the emotions that Twombly generates so maudlin? Well, he's working for the future equivalent of Hallmark, so why not? But if that's so, why does he himself take the sentiments so sincerely? Maybe that's how techies look at human emotions, and it's up to the English majors to gag and look for saving ironies. Still, after years of this syrup, why does he never groan in horror at his own handiwork? Why do his coworkers admire what he does? Why do publishers—who appear like two little gray-haired, bow-tied hobbits fussing over something precious—love what he writes and turn it into a book? These owl-like editors fit a stereotype for book people that might have passed in a William Powell dramatic comedy in 1935, but now? It's got to be a joke. It was probably a joke in 1935. For that matter, why are there still *books* in Twombly's world? I know it's not supposed to be in the far future, but even if it's only 2025, haven't they murdered hard copy yet? It figures, though, that if there are still books in 2025, they'll be this sort of saccharine crap.*

Surely the viewer is meant to raise an eyebrow about this gunk. Surely we are meant to distance ourselves from Twombly. If we buy into these emotions, isn't the joke on us? Don't we pass judgment on ourselves when we tear up at lines like "We are only here briefly, and in this moment I want to allow myself joy"? I'd be relieved if it were a joke on someone, anyone, but if it is a joke, Jonze has an acidic side that most people miss, especially those on whom the joke falls most heavily.

How are we meant to react to the environment in which Twombly works?

---

* In the August 2014 issue of *Wired*—in a special section titled "Creativity Unleashed: A Mobile Manifesto"—the claim is made that the literature of the future can still be creative even if it is written for Twitter: "Literary fiction—a traditional medium with selective gatekeepers—can successfully engage with the way people read online." I don't like these "gatekeepers" any more than *Wired*, but the idea that literary fiction can be replaced by fiction written on Twitter is self-interested and . . . *your adjective here* (mine are all obscene). *Wired* exists in order to calm us about the future: everything will be the same, only better, we're told in issue after issue. Twombly writes fictions that are a little too long for Twitter but have the same relationship to "literary fiction," whatever that is. The owlish gatekeepers let him in, God knows why, so he passes for literary. But when he looks at the finished book in his hand, even he is confused. He doesn't know what to feel or how to react. He doesn't know whether to feel vindicated or scorned. In their different ways, what Jonze and *Wired* allow us to consider is the world as techno-farce.

After Twombly finishes the letter to the older couple, the camera moves back and then pans the room in which he works, revealing that he is far from alone. There is a factory of workers, each at a desk, dictating letters like the one that Twombly has just finished. It is reminiscent of those photographs of the inside of the old Sears building in Chicago, where hundreds and hundreds of female clerks sat at their desks and processed orders by hand—all of them lined up in neat rows as if the factory floor were a circuit board. This scene should be alarming. It should be an expression of horror at the implications of businesses where humans become parts of a larger machine and their boredom has no standing. This warehouse of writers dictating drivel for people lacking their own emotions implies a world of people *with quantified souls.*

Jonze makes us look at this vision, but only briefly. Had he lingered, or panned back and up, the ambiguity of his criticism would have been lost, and it's too early in the film for that. What he reveals, then hides, is deftly done.

Finally, what sort of "meaning" does this first scene set us up for? Most important, how does this scene help us to understand how Jonze expects us to evaluate Twombly?
The most important question in understanding how this film creates meaning is: what are we meant to think about Twombly? Is he a protagonist with whom we are meant to identify? Or is he the object of our amusement? Is he someone—whether

admirable or not—for whom we can feel compassion? In short, is this a romantic comedy or a satire? Is it both? Why did the critical reception of the film miss the satire and focus only on the romance? Worryingly, if it is intended as a satire, does it remain a satire if there is no one capable of getting the joke?

My contention would be that there is nothing in this first scene that should lead us to any conclusion other than that it is a satire. Twombly is an "unreliable narrator." In film as well as novels, we expect the narrator to be a voice that we can trust. Rare is the novel or film whose narrator is evil, or crazy, or stupid. The challenge for readers of works with unreliable narrators is that the reader must constantly make allowances for what they are being told because the narrator is crazy (*Lolita*) or too stupid to see what the reader sees clearly (Ford Madox Ford's *The Good Soldier*). Twombly's point of view is unreliable because he ardently believes in all the things that the filmmaker has just shown us to be false and scary. Sympathize with him if you want, but he's a little stupid.

But there is another possibility—and it is a master stroke: we identify with Twombly because he is more like us than we know; we are critical of him because Jonze forces us to see how corrupted he is; and we feel compassion for him because in important ways he is a victim, just as we all are. This is a terrifying, haunting thing to think: we sympathize with the corrupt who are victims and deserving of our compassion.

A MIDWAY SCENE

About midway through the film, Twombly meets his ex-wife, Catherine (Rooney Mara), to sign papers finalizing their divorce. They meet over lunch, outdoors, at a restaurant for the gentry. (The entire world depicted in this movie is for the gentry. Indeed, it is the world of *Average Is Over*: the poor people have been shipped off to the hinterlands.) His wife is irritable and unhappy. She seems not to think much of her life. Unlike her husband, she is not "seeing someone." This, too, is Jonze's decision, not hers. The fact that she's not seeing anyone puts her isolation in boldface. Then she asks Twombly how he's doing. Great! he says. He's in love. With whom? An operating system, he answers bravely. Earlier in the film Twombly tells one of his male colleagues that he's dating a computer, and without a pause the colleague replies, "Great. Let's have a picnic. Bring her along." Does Twombly expect something similar from Catherine? If he does, he's disappointed, because Catherine's response is scornful in the extreme.

Catherine sees in his admission just the reality that has made her so miserable, so alone: she is living in a world of clones. She now sees in lurid detail the virtual world that Twombly chose over her, and her worst fears are confirmed. She sees that Twombly is living in a fantasy world where everything is virtual-by-nature; Twombly has become an avatar of himself. This is the only moment in the movie where we see someone who aggressively dislikes this brave new world of computers that are better-than-us, this world in which we ourselves have become better than ourselves by becoming virtual (Twombly lives in the cloud, in the Internet of Things, and not on earth). This is why the scene is in the movie—Catherine provides the only human perspective in the film. Twombly has flashbacks of their early romance (adroitly handled by Jonze) while he's sitting at the table with her. In these flashbacks he is nostalgic not only for a lost love, *but for his own barely remembered humanity.*

So, if we are *reading* the film, we should ask: Why has Jonze chosen to include this scene? How does it comment on the rest of the movie? Why is Catherine the only character in the movie who seems to hate this new world? And why does the viewer (if you insist: "why do I") suddenly feel strong agreement with her, as if the willing suspension of disbelief we had granted the movie now felt like we'd been bamboozled into sympathizing with this hyper-digitized future? What could we have been thinking? But then, somehow, as soon as she's gone we're back in Twombly's corner, worrying about how he's going to take this trauma on top of all the other weird shit.

THE OWL SCENE

The image of an enormous and threatening owl plunging down toward Twombly, practically lifting him from the sidewalk, is not subtle. The image comes at a particularly critical moment in the movie: Twombly has just learned that Samantha is going away and that she has had six-hundred-forty-one virtual lovers, a number that would have impressed the Roman empress-whore Messalina. The scene lasts only a few seconds, but it is the one moment in the film that shows what Jonze really thinks. He thinks that Twombly is vulnerable—a prey—to enormously powerful forces that he cannot see or understand. He is a victim.

This calls to mind a similar scene in *Doubt*. For most of that movie, playwright John Patrick Shanley has kept our judgment brilliantly suspended. We like Father Brendan Flynn (Philip Seymour Hoffman) and don't much like the brusque Sister Aloysius Beauvier (Meryl Streep). But we also know that child abuse by priests is a real and serious thing, so Flynn's guilt or innocence remains an open question. But in one brief scene Shanley shows us his real thoughts about Father Flynn. He shows a group of priests, including Flynn, eating dinner. They are the image of gluttony. There are cigars, plenty of booze, and a very bloody-looking piece of meat that they seem to be tearing at. All of Flynn's charm and intelligence are destroyed in that moment. True, we will be returned to uncertainty, but if we have been attentive we now know the truth.

Jonze has said that his film is emotional. I agree. But it is this moment in which a digital owl descends on him, and not the ridiculous bathos of unrequited love with an operating system, that makes the film moving and makes Twombly sympathetic. For he is, sadly, an ordinary man and no match for the forces that oppose him. And neither are we.

•

My conclusion is this: Jonze asks us to imagine a world that is homogeneous, infinitely homogeneous, and for that reason very wrong. He asks us to imagine a science-fictional world where the humans don't have to be harvested by some alien species or dunked in digestive fluid, as in the 2014 film *Under the Skin*. He shows us a world where the entire species has erotically cathected to a reigning order in which people are sucked of life by their own telephones while muttering Hallmark-card banalities. And in all this world there remains one person—the ex, the exocentric one, the last glitch in a system that doesn't need her—with whose skepticism, indignation, and anger we identify for one brief moment before the slow, self-destructive, but inevitable plot (as in "story" but also as in "conspiracy") makes its way to its conclusion.

In the words of the Marxist philosopher Louis Althusser, everyone has been "interpolated" into a nightmare world of zombie nerds—except Catherine. It is she, the only recognizable human in the film, who is *alien*. Why did she turn out so differently? There is no reason. She just happens to be what Althusser called a "bad subject." Unlike *1984*'s Winston Smith, she doesn't have to be reeducated. She's just a minor glitch— the kind that any OS-World might have. This world is a beta version and it will have its Catherines. But she doesn't require a security patch. She can be safely ignored until it's time to debug and bring out a more seamless edition: World.2. Perhaps she will find other bad subjects to conspire with, or love (it amounts to the same thing), or she will just be alienated and infinitely scared and unhappy. Given what the film offers, it seems to me that the second option is more likely.

One last thought: Is it possible that Catherine is the "her" to whom the film's title refers? We assume it is Samantha, but the title is ambiguous. Thinking that "her" is Samantha tends to lead to one reading of the film, an obvious and not very interesting reading in which we take Twombly's love affair seriously. Imagining that "her" refers to Catherine leads to interesting alternatives: the possibility of heterogeneity, of freaks, united mutants, and resistance.

Is this the subtle yet corrosive film that Jonze was trying to make? Or is *Her* nothing more than an homage to techno-lust, romantic clichés, and generalized stupidity—the movie that Spaeth saw, in other words? If I'm correct, those viewers who bought into the emotions of the movie, who love their smartphones, who see sexting and any future forms of virtual sex as an inevitable and, in any case, a welcome extension of iPorn, who were deeply moved by the film and Liked and Faved it in affirmation—well, these viewers watched a film that *made it possible for them to condemn themselves.*

And then there is the ex, Catherine, the faithful captive in Babylon. If, like me, you conclude that she is the real hero of the film, *you will feel like her when reading the reviews that praise the film for its emotional content.* You will feel her isolation and you will emerge feeling what she feels: frightened and outcast.

In the final scene, Twombly messages Catherine and sends a heartfelt piece of sappy schmaltz *identical to the letters he writes at work*. This scene takes us back to the very first image in the film where Twombly is dictating a letter for the older couple. In other words, he's writing a beautifully handwritten letter *for himself*. By balancing the first scene with the last, Jonze creates a powerful structural unity, and makes his intention unmistakable. There is no inner life left in Twombly. He is now, truly, *one of them*, as if he's been body-snatched. That's how Jonze means us to feel, like Catherine: she, the last human standing, is being pursued by aliens who look like humans—who look like her husband—and who are trying to persuade her to give up, come over, be happy, and become one of us.

Immediately after sending this message, Twombly and his friend Amy (Amy Adams) sit on top of their apartment building watching the sun setting over sterile skyscrapers. Both of them are on the rebound from bad breakups with their software, and yet neither of them has a clue about how they might be romantically interested in each other, even though that's what the standard romantic comedy script calls for here. We *expect* Amy and Theodore to find each other, human at last, and kiss. And that is exactly what *doesn't* happen. If they had kissed, *Her* would have had a more optimistic meaning. Yes, there is technology all around, but in the end we are still human. In the end we find each other, in spite of the machines. But that is *not* what Jonze chose to portray. That is *not* what he leaves us with.

This scene is meant to rhyme with the earlier scene of Twombly at the beach with Samantha. He goes to the right place with his smartphone, and to the wrong place with a human. Shouldn't we understand this as irony? The really disturbing thing is that except for Catherine no other character in the film can see this irony, just as few members of the movie's critics have seen it. True, Jonze doesn't hammer home the moral; he allows it to remain ambiguous (with the exception of the owl). By doing so, he makes it possible for the audience to get it terribly wrong, but in a very revealing way. This movie is not a Rorschach and it's not a selfie—it's an autopsy. We look at the corpse, all of its parts clearly displayed, but all we can think to do is comb our hair, check e-mail, and upload a new Instagram photo.

Zounds!

Or perhaps it's *my* reading that's in the spirit of a selfie, a reflection of my own attitude toward technology. But can *all* of this be in the film by accident? When something is so consistently developed from first to last, critics usually assume that it is the representation of something that the artist *thinks*. From the perspective I have described, *Her* is not a melodrama—it's a satire of a rare order: it breaks our hearts.

And that hug with Audie Cornish? It's a prank. The joke is on us if we take it seriously.

•

Virtual reality is coming, and you're going to jump into it.
—Farhad Manjoo, "State of the Art,"
The New York Times, April 3, 2014

•

FROM SEX-POT TO SEX-BOT

There is an obvious narrative line in *Her* that Jonze declines to develop. In the fullness of their young love, Twombly and his plastic fantastic lover Samantha lament the fact that they can't sleep together. They have a virtual romance, but it's a genitally "stand-down" relationship, as a military man might say. To correct this, Samantha takes the initiative and recruits a sex surrogate (Isabella, played by Portia Doubleday) as a stand-in for herself. The idea is, one supposes, that while he is screwing Isabella he is thinking about his computer.*

But, wait, hadn't we seen Twombly interacting with a 3-D smart-ass video game avatar while Samantha watched and laughed along at the avatar's crude jokes? So if most viewers are like yours truly, they're asking, "Hey, why go to all the mess of another actual human when she could simply pick a body like she picked a name and create a holographic avatar of herself using whoever—Marilyn Chambers in her prime or (why not?) Gina Lollobrigida! The young Lauren Bacall! Think crazy!"

That is a path not taken by Jonze, although I wonder why. Because one of the big stories on the tech scene in 2013 was Facebook's takeover of Oculus VR's virtual-reality goggles. And one of the big stories about Oculus in 2014 concerned its usefulness in enabling virtual sex. And of course there's an

---

* This puts me in mind of a Sir Doug Sahm Texas Tornadoes song, "Who Were You Thinkin' of When We Were Makin' Love Last Night." It continues, "You got more out of it than I put into it last night."

accompanying narrative strikingly like Tyler Cowen's script for the economy of the future: VR is the *future of sex*.

A few tech companies have come a way with this, but the way they've come has mostly opened them to ridicule. Take the case of Tenga, a Japanese manufacturer of disposable male sex toys.* In the fall of 2013, Tenga joined with a game developer and Oculus Rift technology to produce a virtual sex experience in which an *anime* female (her raised buttocks, at the least) is synchronized with a frightening hand job robot (a contraption that looks like an invitation to put one's virile member into a vegetable juicer) to deliver the latest in self-consolation. (The robot is a first-generation creation of the new field of "teledildonics," awful as that sounds.) Tenga CEO Tsuneki Sato commented, "I think in the future, the virtual real will become more real than actual real sex." Elsewhere, SugarDVD, a sort of porn Netflix, is preparing to use motion-capture technology and hyper-real HD representations of actual humans to produce "interactive adult experiences."

In the March 2015 "Sex in the Digital Age" issue of *Wired*, Peter Rubin put it this way:

> In VR, the frame of detachment disappears, and fantasy effectively does too. You're not watching a scene anymore; you're inhabiting it. And by being there, you're implicated in whatever's happening.

---

* Disposable. Yes. That's clear enough.

For the most part, this emerging scene is food for blog thought and not for the old-school analog media. And so far bloggers on sites like *Motherboard, BV: VentureBeat,* and *PC-Gamer* have taken the high road about the morality of such things. It's not all rebel yells. In particular, they have been troubled by the tradeoff of losing the smells and tastes of sex versus the boon of never being rejected, humiliated, betrayed, or abandoned.* There is also the "bowling alone" theme of our ever more isolated lives. But, as Jeffrey Grubb points out in an illuminating post for *VentureBeat,* there are even darker concerns. Will this technology be used to create the virtual experience of murdering someone? Will our own images be captured by stalkers and those otherwise obsessed and put through motion-capture technology so that anyone can have sex with Scarlett Johansson—or you—any time they want? Your spittin' image a virtual sex slave!

Grubb continues:

> Why would you ever suffer through a blind date or setting up an OKCupid profile when you can get exactly what you want whenever you want it without any effort with the help of your Oculus Rift?
>
> For that matter, why go and do anything? Why would

---

* This technology is the true revenge of the nerds. They've grown tired of getting rejected and laughed at by the cool kids. They have two choices for revenge. First, they could get the long, black raincoats and start hoarding guns and munitions. Very few, thanks to God, are actually up for this action. Or, second, they could use their real strength, computer programming, to create a world of sex that they can dominate. This is what they've done. And now they've made it so that even the cool kids want virtual sex. Everybody gotta have it!

you travel the world? . . . You can do all of that from the comfort of your own home while possibly avoiding anything unpleasant or unpredictable.

What Grubb is attempting to describe is the techno-capitalist sublime: a consumer fantasy of de-materialization.[7] No more stinky bodies and no more dangerous bodily fluids. As director Luc Moullet observed in his short film *Toujours Moins*, the consequence of our ever-enlarging robot world is: *always less.*

Always less human.

#STEM-Bot

LEGO: THE SOLUTION TO THE STEM CRISIS!

The controversy over a renewed emphasis on STEM (science, technology, engineering, and math) at all levels of education is broadly known. As President Obama put it in 2010: "[Our] leadership tomorrow depends on how we educate our students today—especially in science, technology, engineering and math." According to Lego Education, the secret to a successful STEM education is not in common standards and teaching to the test, but in robotics. Lego's "Mindstorms Education with TETRIX" allows students to build robots to bring STEM to life, and inspire them to take a more experiential and lasting interest in science and math. "Based on an easy-to-use robotics technology, this engaging platform provides an inspiring, full teaching solution."

"A solution to what?" you might ask. Why, a solution to the Education Crisis. This crisis, another piece of masterful storytelling, maintains that there are not enough American students being prepared in science and math to take up the bounty of career opportunities offered by Apple, Google, and other high-tech businesses. That is why, the story goes, so many jobs in technology have been sent overseas, especially to China. But, as David Sirota has effectively argued in *Salon*, the fact is that American universities are already producing far more STEM-oriented graduates than American businesses hire. According to Sirota, the real purpose of the crisis myth—and the real point of the monumental effort being made to revamp school curriculums—is "acquiescence."

> In beginning to construct this kind of pedagogy, our mandarins are not coincidentally promoting a key part of the educational ideology of their Chinese counterparts. No, not the part of that ideology that is focused on training high-tech workers—the part that prioritizes obedience. [Chinese] educational methods teach Chinese workers never to question their station, demand basic rights, or ask for better conditions.

Beyond the frustration of critics like Sirota and a few unhappy educators and humanists, most people don't see the problem. Most folks are pragmatic about it and see the emphasis on STEM as merely the inevitable consequence of "a changing world," something no one really has control over, not even the president of the United States. Certainly, to see STEM as a conspiracy between capitalism and science, as Sirota does, is paranoid, right? If the economy is becoming more dependent on technology, and if the jobs of the future are going to require sophistication in science and math, well, then that's what our children ought to study, especially if the cost of educating them is going to put the family into sizable debt for two decades after graduation. After all, isn't it our responsibility to "prepare students for the future"?

And yet for STEM's advocates it doesn't seem sufficient to say that the study of science and math is an economic necessity. As Sirota shows, the economic argument cannot easily succeed by itself without seeming callous. After all, who believes that future prosperity should require competing with what the Chinese have: low pay, twelve-hour days, and the abandonment of all human and labor rights? Even granting the importance of being able to compete in global markets, who would willingly consent to such a scenario in the West?

Which is to say that it's a bit of a hard sell.

Yet hard sell or no, ideology's chore is to manufacture consent even to this brutal reality by telling certain stories, and science has an important contribution to make. What science's popular representatives—its ideologues—argue is that beyond the brutal and coercive economic arguments for STEM there is moral necessity. Science justifies the increased emphasis on the study of STEM disciplines by saying that not only are they the only certain means to a decent job, but they are also superior to (by which they mean "truer" than) the humanistic disciplines, and they are certainly *infinitely* superior to any education that includes religion. The two critical words that guarantee the moral superiority of a STEM-based education are "skepticism" and "reason." A thinking human, the argument goes, should be skeptical of all nonrational forms of knowledge (religion, metaphysics, art); and a thinking human should always strive to be rational, although what exactly "rational" means is never said. This is the explicit argument of one of the most sought-after speakers on the STEM circuit, Michael Shermer, who presented a talk titled "Do You Believe in Myths, Urban Legends & Superstitions?" at the X-STEM festival in November 2013.

What is X-STEM?

> X-STEM—presented by Northrop Grumman Foundation and MedImmune—is an Extreme STEM symposium for elementary through high school students featuring interactive presentations by an exclusive group of visionaries who aim to empower and inspire kids about careers in science, technology, engineering and mathematics (STEM).*

Taken together, the economic necessity of STEM and the moral necessity of science as skepticism/rationalism have achieved the status of that which is established, verified, and proven. It's as if we've been programmed, like one of Tyler Cowen's intelligent machines, to think that if we want to prosper we must study one of the STEM fields, which is a good thing in any case because it is based in our freedom from superstition and in that quintessentially human trait: our ability to reason. So don't object if the world becomes narrower, the hours longer, the living conditions cramped, and the tasks boring and repetitive—at least you will be employed and no one will believe that the image of Mother Mary has appeared on the top of a grilled cheese sandwich.

Hurrah!

---

* Extreme STEM! How cool that must sound to sixth graders. Like doing a 180 off a picnic table!

OUR GULLIBLE SKEPTICS

But isn't it true that science is not skeptical in *all* things, just those modes of thought that aren't like it? And isn't it also true that the arguments of science advocates are often not particularly rational, if part of what that term means is "not dependent on unproven presuppositions"? There's plenty of evidence to support both of these suggestions in popular journals and academic studies, but this is rarely noticed and almost never commented on. Shermer writes a regular column for *Scientific American* called "Skeptic: Viewing the World with a Rational Eye." What is remarkable about many of Shermer's columns—beyond his insufferable delight in being endlessly rational—is their dependence on unexamined assumptions. In other words, their irrationality.

For example, in the May 2014 issue of *SA*, Shermer argued that "before all learning, an infant's mind has a sense of right and wrong." He supports his claim with two pieces of evidence. The first is from a YouTube video gone viral in which an assailant pushes a woman off a subway platform. A bystander attempts to prevent this, but he is too late.

> In a flash, two neural networks in the rescuer's brain are engaged to act: help a fellow human in trouble or punish the perpetrator? What's a moral primate to do?

Because no train is coming, Shermer explains, the bystander is able to do both. He "coldcocks" the culprit and pulls the woman to safety. For Shermer, this incident illustrates our "multifaceted moral nature": "Be nice to those who help us and our kin and kind, and punish those who hurt us and our kin and kind." But don't make the mistake of thinking that our valiant bystander *chose* to do the coldcocking. If there was any choosing to be done his neural networks did it all. He merely acted as a sort of soft-tissue robot accomplice.

Shermer also appeals to the work of Yale psychologist Paul Bloom, author of the 2013 book *Just Babies: The Origins of Good and Evil.* Bloom claims that we are "naturally endowed" with a moral sense that allows us to distinguish between kind and cruel actions. As Shermer describes it:

> In Bloom's laboratory, a one-year-old baby watched puppets enact a morality play. One puppet rolled a ball to a second puppet who passed the ball back. The first puppet then rolled the ball to a different puppet, who ran off with the ball. The baby was next given a choice between taking a treat away from the "nice" puppet or the "naughty" one. As Bloom predicted, the infant removed the treat from the naughty puppet—which is what most babies do in this experiment. But for this little moralist, removing a positive reinforcement (the treat) was not enough. "The boy then leaned over and smacked this puppet on the head," Bloom recounts. In his inchoate moral mind, punishment was called for.

I want to examine Shermer's language and his assumptions, but first I have to wonder about the babies involved in this experiment. Were they made aware of possible negative consequences of their participation? Might they not at some future point in their development find that they have an irrational and mysterious fear of puppets? Will they find themselves pummeling innocent others who for some reason remind them of the evil puppets? And how will these experiences affect their own moral nature? It has always been my understanding that we should tell our children "It's not nice to hit," but now we're supposed to cheer the arrival of Baby Vengeance and say, "It's okay to hit when you are punishing evildoers." Sounds more like something the Taliban might tell their children.

I'm sorry. I've stooped to satire again.

Satire aside, I am astonished at Shermer's easy use of terms like "natural endowment," "moral nature," and our "moral sense"—terms that he uses as if they required no explanation at all. Unfortunately, these terms are fictions or, in Vaihinger's language, "an expedient form of error." These are words that seem meaningful simply because they are familiar. Like the words "imagination" or "conscience," they are placeholders for things we might intuit in some provisional way but don't really *know* at all. Coming from rationalists and scientists, it seems a bit like cheating: everything must be empirical/logical except *their* presuppositions. The truth is that presupposing the existence of our "moral nature" has the same logical validity as presupposing the existence of God.

Perhaps I'm quibbling about terminology. So let me ask: What is it about what these babies do, or what the subway avenger did, that makes their actions *moral*? Why is "moral" the right word? It has been a commonplace (and a fiction) for more than a century to suppose that morality emerges from the familial setting and the need to care for and protect the human infant. Shermer's version of this story is to say, "Be nice to those who help us and our kin and kind, and punish those who hurt us and our kin and kind." For Shermer, this conclusion is not the result of the development of human culture but of evolutionary biology.

But if he's being consistent about the evolutionary logic, shouldn't he include the behavior of other animals, like the redwing blackbirds that dive at my bike helmet when I pass a nest because I'm not kin and threaten their kind? Should we call their aggression moral too? Or consider Benjamin Kilham's 2013 book *Out on a Limb: What Black Bears Have Taught Me About Intelligence and Intuition*, in which he describes how black bears use punishment to enforce codes of conduct. Like Bloom's infants, the bears understand the value of a good smack to the head, but Kilham has better sense than to conflate animal behavior with morality.

To be moral in any humanly meaningful sense is to enter into a self-conscious and ever-shifting grammar of conduct that a given community has agreed to live by. The earliest moral documents remaining to us—like the Maxims of Ptahhotep (2000 BC)—suggest that morality begins not with reflexive acts of punishment or protection, but with the *abstraction* of the accused and the injured taken to an entirely new level of human interaction that the Egyptians called *Maat*, or "righteousness,"

"justice," and "truth." *Maat* expressed a sense of the moral order of the nation and the cosmos. The crucial thing to see in
it is that *Maat* could not exist *until* it could be expressed as
moral "sentence," as a maxim. *Maat* didn't exist until there was
language for it.

And babies don't do maxims!

Of course, there was no shortage of punishing and protecting in early civilization, but that was not *Maat*. As a state vizier,
Ptahhotep advised, "Be gracious when thou hearest the speech
of the petitioner. Do not assail him until he has cleaned out
his belly of what he thought to say to thee. He who is suffering wrong desires that his heart be cheered to accomplish that
on account of which he has come." And then, charmingly, "It is
an ornament of the heart to hear kindly."

In other words, the anger of the petitioner is not to be expressed through "coldcocking" the accused. The anger of the
petitioner has its moment in a courtroom. This is why our juries are not composed of "kin and kind"; they are made up
of "twelve men, good and true." This is how we have agreed
to negotiate justice in our culture. Without this process of
negotiation between a party that claims it has been harmed
and a party that claims it is innocent of said harm, we have
only whatever morality can be found in force and the "right of
conquest."

In the case Shermer presents us with, the subway assailant
might in fact have been found *not* guilty because he was cognitively diminished at the moment of the assault or mentally

incompetent to stand trial. I would assume that most people who push others from subway platforms are mentally deficient in some way. What Shermer submits for our admiration is an act of vigilantism. Had this coldcocking continued with a more thorough beating, beyond what was needed for detaining the perpetrator, the bystander himself would have been guilty of assault or worse, just as the shop owner (or cop) who shoots a fleeing thief can be tried for murder. The gut-level approval of punching a "bad guy" might go over well with the booyah crowd on YouTube, but it shouldn't be persuasive to the readers of *Scientific American*.

Shermer concludes his piece by saying, "This is why the constitutions of our nations should be grounded in the constitution of our nature." Thank God they're not. Happily for us, there is a superior wisdom that is the product of millennia of human experience with organized life. This wisdom is quite unlike anything Shermer may have in mind. Morality is actually the human *objection* to evolution, to nature as something "red in tooth and claw." The arrival of this objection is the arrival of humanity. It is something like this: when biological evolution generated the capacity for abstract reason in humans, it also generated the human capacity for *objecting* to the "logic" of evolution—"survival of the fittest." At a certain point in the development of human cultures, we decided that we were going to try not to progress solely through violence (survival "by the sword" or what the ancient world called "the right of conquest").

Needless to say, this is a human dispute that is far from settled.

The error in Shermer's thinking begins with his presupposition that there is something called morality or justice. There is not. In its simplest term, what Ptahhotep called *Maat* was an agreement among humans not to harm each other, an agreement that was enforced by the state vizier, and beyond him, ambivalently, the pharaoh's police apparatus. The Greek Stoic philosopher Epicurus arrived at the same conclusion. He wrote: "Justice never is anything in itself, but in the dealings of men with one another in any place whatever and at any time it is a kind of compact not to harm or be harmed." Any religious or metaphysical claims about the nature of justice are just "empty sounds," and so, I would add, are claims that our neural circuits make us moral.

The *political* point of Shermer's exercise in moral logic is not in its advocacy of retributive violence; it is in the fact that it removes the question of morality from its traditional specialists—theologians, philosophers like Ptahhotep, and artists. Shermer is saying that we don't need those disciplines because science can provide us with better, simpler answers. There is no need to study philosophy in order to understand morality, and oh, by the way, there's no great consequence in dropping philosophy altogether because there will not be much in the way of gainful employment for philosophers in the economy of the future. Therefore, you should study science, technology, and math—fields where there is both a salary and truth. Shermer is a techno-philistine.

The guilty secret here is that these easy conclusions are themselves harming "kin and kind." Shermer's putative reasonableness is a form of immorality because it hides the harm it does. STEM funnels children into a high-tech economy that constricts their life chances and opportunities even as it conceals this very fact. And even those who have an aptitude for the STEM disciplines ought to feel like their options are punishingly narrow. As Cowen squarely put it, fit your skills to the needs of intelligent machines, or else. Adding insult to injury, apologists like Shermer—"America's skeptic in residence"—then follow and put a veneer of science and reason over the whole mess.

We should not be misled. What Shermer helps provide intellectual cover for is, to employ Herbert Marcuse's word, "one-dimensional." As Marcuse wrote in *One-Dimensional Man*: "A comfortable, smooth, reasonable, democratic unfreedom prevails in advanced industrial civilization, a token of technical progress."

•

A great many people think they are thinking when they are merely rearranging their prejudices.

—WILLIAM JAMES

•

I ALREADY KNEW THAT

There's a sense in which we don't need philosophers like Marcuse to explain to us what we already know well. Especially at the more sophisticated levels of the culture, among tech workers and their entourage, we're well aware that the STEM fix is in, and that the robots are standing behind our backs wielding a board with a nail through it. Consider this "Savage Chickens" cartoon from 2013:

The fact that it is a robot, and not a foreman, that is enforcing alienated labor is revealing: the cartoonist understands—and we signal our understanding when we laugh—that the economic realities described by people like Tyler Cowen and Michael Shermer are both real and oppressive.

But there is something troubling about this cartoon. Unlike Marcuse, the cartoonist doesn't seem to *resent* this state of affairs. How seriously should we take the loss of the art this chicken produces at his easel? If that's lost, so what? Same for our efforts: if they're lost, so what? Just the fact that we're asked to identify with a cartoon chicken tends to diminish us in our own eyes. And as for the robot, he is a merely comic reduction of whatever force it is that compels our obedience. Doesn't this seem like the kind of consciousness-raising that's done on the way back to sleep? It's not about resistance; it's about acquiescence. It assures us that, no, you're not crazy. Being ruled by robots is indeed a fucked-up situation, but it's the situation, it's reality, as David Brooks would scold. So go ahead and sigh.*

The chicken sighs, we all sigh . . . but then we go back to work.

I first saw our oppressed chicken on a Facebook page called Title Wave, where one commenter responded to the cartoon with "Hanging this up in my cubicle." The commenter was being ironic (he knew that hanging it up in his cubicle would merely confirm the condition the cartoon describes), but there was a bleaker lesson in his remark: his gesture was identical in its futility to the gesture of the cartoon itself. The cartoon is hip (hip to the idea that the creative economy is just another form of voluntary servitude), and the audience is hip (or they wouldn't get the humor), but it's the sort of hipness that Mark Crispin Miller, invoking Kierkegaard's idea of "aesthetic irony," calls the "hipness unto death."

---

* The cartoonist, Doug Savage, has a 2011 book titled *Savage Chickens: A Survival Kit for Life in the Coop.* The cartoons are all drawn on yellow sticky notes. Savage claims that by day he "edits software manuals in the dark recesses of a giant corporation." It's worth remembering that for Cowen these are the *good* jobs, the jobs worth desiring.

For Kierkegaard, aesthetic irony merely transforms boredom into something interesting by using irony, paradox, will-
fulness—all the ploys used by Oscar Wilde's hapless dandies.
But this irony—attractive though it may be, relief though it
may be, funny though it may be, because ordinarily we are not
allowed to complain about our boredom—is finally a form of
despair because it does not take responsibility for the fact that
this boredom/oppression is social. It is not only happening to
the chicken or the techie-hipster; it is also happening to others
to whom we *should* owe, mmm . . . solidarity? Loyalty? *Care?*

The cartoon appeals to us only in our isolation. In other
words, it appeals to us only in our defeat. It is just one of a thousand micro-stimulations delivered to us in the course of a day—
in this case, on Facebook—by our machines. Deeper attention
and any orientation toward caring has been stripped away.

So, chickens of the world, unite! You have nothing to lose
but your fetters!

REALITY! (LOUD SHOUTS)

Michael Shermer claims that he "views the world with a rational eye." The truth is that he is a metaphysician. He is one of
those who believe, as Henri Bergson wrote in "The Evolution
of Life," that the "living body might be treated by some superhuman calculator in the same mathematical way as our solar
system." He is a mechanist and a materialist and therefore a
metaphysician. Bergson again: "The mechanistic instinct of

the mind is stronger than reason, stronger than immediate experience. The metaphysician that we each carry unconsciously within us . . . has its fixed requirements, its ready-made explanations, its irreducible propositions."

Shermer, along with so many other science ideologues, seems perfectly content with these ready-made explanations. He is also confident that what he describes in his *Scientific American* column is something comfortably close to reality. But he does not describe reality; he describes what the twentieth-century physicist and cosmologist Arthur Eddington called "reality (loud cheers)." Shermer's work describes reality only in the sense that he writes for *SA*, whose readers have a strong tendency to be happy to hear that reality is mechanical (loud cheers).

Eddington did not discount the results of the experimental methods agreed to by the scientific community (a "symposium"). These results can be made "ever purer," but they never entirely escape their dependence on the actions and beliefs of the community. For example, scientists apply a traditional metric for determining that a causal link is more than a case of bias or chance: they apply what statisticians call a 95 percent confidence limit. In other words, a claim will be considered established if it can show that the odds of the claim being false are no more than one in twenty. But the 95 percent level has nothing to do with nature; it is a convention and the topic of some controversy among statisticians. For Eddington, science gets purer as this "confidence level" increases but it doesn't necessarily become truer.

On the other hand, Eddington entirely dismisses truth

claims that seem to participate in the scientific symposium but are really only expressions of "sentiment." He writes: "The truth we seek in science is the truth about an external world propounded as the theme of study, and is not bound up with any opinion as to the status of that world." The idea that the Higgs boson is the "God particle" is a good example of "sentiment," as is Shermer's conclusion that "morality" is to be found in neural circuitry. This is a crucial if forgotten distinction for contemporary science because *all* the popular proclamations about religion, robotics, free will, creativity, consciousness, morality, and so on that are made by New Atheists, neuroscience evangelicals, and science journalists like Shermer are what Eddington would call "sentimental," not "scientific." They do not present us with "reality" but with "reality (loud cheers)."

Eddington's essay "Reality, Causation, Science and Mysticism" is a tremendously illuminating work that brings together science, philosophy, and even spirit in a way that science ideologues like Shermer are incapable of. For Eddington, Shermer's "moral materialism" works only if most of human experience is disdained. He writes: "Recognizing that the physical world is entirely abstract and without 'actuality' apart from its linkage to consciousness, we restore consciousness to the fundamental position instead of representing it as an inessential complication occasionally found in the midst of inorganic nature at a late stage of evolutionary history." It is thrilling to see this perspective coming from a legendary figure in science and cosmology. But where is it now? Forgotten? Forbidden? Inconvenient? One thing is for certain: if it were present, it would make Michael Shermer's as-ifs most implausible.

SORRY, BUT WE'RE STILL USING THAT

Unacknowledged assumptions operate at the very highest level of Anglo-American intellectual culture. For example, the permanent war over the existence of free will, which pits science against the humanities. The science position argues that there is no free will—only biologically and neurologically determined actions. (The subway protector, whose heroism was the result of actions taken by his neural circuitry, is a prime example.) In one formulation—an extreme one usually associated with the physiologist Benjamin Libet—our brains "know" what we're going to do before we do.

The humanist position tends to argue that there is free will in one form or another. But usually the argument can be reduced to a tautology along these lines: "I have the subjective experience of *intention*. I can *choose*. I can behave randomly if I *will* it."*

What should be self-evident but doesn't seem to be is the idea that both terms—freedom and will—are fictions first, and the two terms brought together are all that much more a fiction. The idea of free will is a heuristic, a provisional way of invoking something we think we feel and that we know we need if we're

---

* I leave to the side (and not just for the moment because I have no intention of returning to it) the so-called "compatibilist" option in which neuroscience and volition are found to be compatible. Obviously.

going to continue to live in what we (again, fictively) call civil society. In short, it is neither true nor false, and we neither have it nor don't have it—it is simply useful or not, desired or not.

This is a position that science itself once thought to be true: that what we take to be reality is a "mental construct." For example, the particle physicist Sir James Jeans, in the concluding chapter of his book *Physics and Philosophy*, has this to say regarding the "reality" of electric and magnetic forces:

> The physical theory of relativity has now shown that electric and magnetic forces are not real at all; they are mere mental constructs of our own, resulting from our rather misguided efforts to understand the motions of the particles.

In Jeans's view, the vulgar mechanistic view of reality—in which reality is "clearly defined particles clearly located in space and executing clear-cut motions"—is Victorian. On the other hand, the world we live in, the world that was inaugurated by relativity and quantum physics, is not an either/or world. Like the famous instance of the beam of light that is both particle and wave, it's a both/and world. Jeans quotes Bertrand Russell:

> Everything that we can directly observe of the physical world happens inside our heads, and consists of *mental* events in at least one sense of the word *mental*. It also consists of events which form part of the physical world. The development of this point of view will lead us to the conclusion that the distinction between mind and matter is illusory. The stuff of the world may be called physical or mental or both or neither as we please; in fact the words serve no purpose.

Does the scientific community continue to recognize these distinctions? Apparently not, especially if the scientist in question also happens to be—like Shermer—a libertarian ideologue and TED Talk celebrity. (That's Technology Entertainment Design Talk, for the uninitiated.) Science ideologues continue to tell a story that is both outdated and untrue, and in so doing, they betray their own intellectual history.

The concept of free will is *necessary* in the sense that for humans in the West to continue to participate in our common creation—civil society—we must maintain an allegiance to the idea that we are *free* to choose for good or bad. This gets endlessly complicated when the idea of free will becomes enmeshed with ideologies concerning morality, law, and punishment—especially when a society like our own is based upon the notion of "property," the ethics of work, and the repayment of debt. For centuries, English debtors were sent to the Clink, and thieves could be and were sent to the gallows for pinching a hat. Their crimes were said to be willful even though the context in which they acted was unjust. Something called "free will" cannot be separated out from this byzantine and coercive social context as if it were a freestanding thing.

And yet that is what many critics do. For example, in his August 2012 "Skeptic" column in *SA*, Michael Shermer tries to test for the presence/absence of free will through the example of having to choose between a steak or salmon dinner. Shermer and nearly all other debaters treat steak or salmon arguments as if they were the salient point and not a reductio ad absurdum.* Shermer's argument is atomistic: free will is about discrete acts of choosing; it is not affected by the infinite flux and flow of the history of human societies. In Shermer's view, no deed possesses a past or a meaningful context. In thinking this way, Shermer prepares the way for the "emerging field of robot morality" in which, say, a robotic car must choose between braking and swerving when approaching a collision, or an autonomous robot soldier must decide whether or not to use its weapons.

From the perspective of science, free will is either an illusion or it is something that can be accounted for in scientific terms. Actually, even if it is an illusion, science should be able to account for it because the creation of illusions is every bit as much a part of cognition as is the action of free will. (There is already a neuroscience of habit; can the neuroscience of illusion be far behind? Will the neuroscience of illusion also study the illusions of neuroscience?) And certainly a scientific description of any behavior is possible in the sense that there are always things that can be measured: in the moment that a person feels compelled to choose between steak and salmon, MRIs can be captured, the heart rate monitored, digestive fluids analyzed, statistics regarding subjective experience gathered, etc. Beyond that, the science becomes dependent on prose approximations,

---

* This hard choice between salmon and steak—rather than between macaroni and cheese and hamburger helper—makes credible Nietzsche's observation that "freedom of will is the invention of *ruling* classes."

probabilities, and conjecture—*as-ifs*. But that's not what science claims it does—even though that is exactly what it does.

•

> You must remember that by the time that science becomes a
> closed—that is, computerizable—project, it is not science
> anymore.
>   —JACOB BRONOWSKI

•

The tallest tale told by science is that its war against quasi-
religious concepts like free will is made possible by something
they call "reason" or "rationality." My question is: why isn't reason also governed by biological determinism? Why isn't reason
something that happens in the brain before we become conscious of it? No, science proselytizers wear Reason like a badge,
a medallion showing their superiority to all those many forms
of the irrational that they scorn. The idea of Reason is privileged, given pride of place over empty concepts like faith, love,
and free will. It is a transcendental signifier. It is a phallus with
bright ribbons dangling, and we're supposed to grab one and
dance around it. Reason is the one term that is immune from
rational critique. The claim that Reason is something True,
while free will is something false, is only another instance of
social authority saying, "It's this way because we, your superi-
ors, say so."

Loud cheers!

•

Why not look at it this way: We may not entirely know what "freedom" is or what it means, but that does not mean that people are going to stop wanting it and fighting for it. As Hegel put it, our desire for freedom is our Spirit. We have chosen it with an existential passion. We have made a decision; we have made a commitment. We are for it even if we don't know what it is. Like the "Spirit of '76," freedom is a story we have committed ourselves to *as if* our lives depended on it. And they obviously do depend on it. The fact that we don't completely understand what freedom means changes nothing. It is what we *want* (both lack and desire). Freedom is our existential wager.

In the meantime, in spite of science's critique of free will and its illusions about reason, we don't dare abandon the ideas of freedom and reason because, sorry, civil society is still using them.

We're not done with them yet.

CONCILIATING THE MYSTERIANS

The September 2014 issue of *Harper's Magazine* contains a major statement on the topic of free will by the eminent biologist E. O. Wilson.[8] Wilson is optimistic that science is close to solving the problem of consciousness/free will (which he regards, correctly, as the same problem), and he offers several very different scenarios for how this solution will be achieved. Unfortunately, like a juggler who finds that all his balls have frozen in midair, his conclusion seems to be that

all the scenarios lead to truth, never mind how incompatible
they are.

Wilson begins with this curious claim:

> [Neuroscientists] are set on discovering the physical basis of
> consciousness, of which free will is a part. No scientific quest
> is more important to humanity.

I say that this is a curious way to begin and yet it is also
typical of the proclamations made by popular science writers.
It is baffling to say that consciousness has a "part" called free
will. In philosophy, this is called a "distinction without a difference." We are not talking about the electron as part of an atom,
and we are certainly not talking about toes as part of the foot.
It is not possible to describe how the two terms are the same but
different without feeling like a Trinitarian trying to describe
how God can be one and three. In short, distinctions such as
the one Wilson is making here are not remotely scientific. God
knows what they are, but they are not the result of causal explanations coming from empirically established laws. Free will
is not a part of consciousness.

Wilson makes no effort to define this thing, consciousness/
free will, that scientists are said to be looking for the physical
basis of. We all have the habit of employing the words, and
we know what they mean by custom, but science is not supposed to begin with habit and custom. The words "consciousness" and "free will" are common currency, coin of the realm,
but they cannot be an object for scientific study unless, at the

very least, the words are defined so that we have some sort of idea what we're looking at. But they can't be defined because they're not things, they are fictions, useful fictions that change as needs require.

Yet for popularizers like Wilson, such matters don't have to be empirical in order for science to weigh in on them. This is so because the scientific method is not only a method; *it is also a morality*. The simple fact that Wilson is a scientist gives him the moral authority to invoke science even when what he's looking at is not open to empirical procedures. It has become *customary* for science ideologues (or "science communicators," as they would prefer to be known) to make pronouncements on every manner of thing and still feel that the moral weight of their Method is standing behind them—even when it's not, even when it can't. Worse, science's moral authority, like any morality enforced hierarchically, enjoys the privilege of "indiscussability." To challenge the right of science to weigh in on free will is to provoke indignation and high dudgeon, not reflection.

Further, why claim that the physical basis of consciousness is the most important scientific "quest"? I'll let the *Star Trek* melodrama of questing pass, but how could finding the physical basis of consciousness be the most important scientific chore, let's call it, for the future of humanity? More important than what? Than finding a non-polluting source of energy? Than getting the world of infectious diseases the hell off our collective back? This isn't science and it sure isn't philosophy. It's loose talk.

Wilson then acknowledges that until recently consciousness has been a problem for philosophy, but philosophy has
failed and its place has been taken by science. In his book *Consilience*, Wilson writes: "Philosophy, the contemplation of the
unknown, is a shrinking dominion. We have the common goal
of turning as much philosophy as possible into science." Here
he joins a legion of philosophy-hating scientists led by Richard
Dawkins, Lawrence Krauss, and Stephen Hawking.

> I don't believe it too harsh to say that the history of philoso-
> phy when boiled down consists mainly of failed models of
> the brain.

That *is* boiled down. Boiled dry might be the more accurate
way of putting it. The central story of the history of philosophy is the failure to model the brain? When you're a famous
scientist like E. O. Wilson, do you get to say anything that
pops into your head, or that reaffirms a prejudice, and expect
that it will be taken with a straight face? Let me clear this up:
philosophy has never been interested in the brain. It has been
deeply interested in mind or spirit (Hegel's *geist*), and it has
been deeply interested in the difference between reason (*ver-
nunft*) and understanding (*verstand*). Kant did indeed offer
a model of the categories of the Understanding—a schematic
that he called the "transcendental deduction" in the *Critique
of Pure Reason*—but that has nothing to do with the brain,
especially since we are uncertain about just what a brain is. Is
it just the three pounds of walnut-shaped soft tissue inside of

the bony carapace of the skull? Should it include the nervous system without which it is not much more than a crenulated nut? Should it include the intestines, where bacteria create 80 percent of the neurotransmitter serotonin? Should it also include the stimuli itself, what Kant called "sensual intuition"?* But somehow for Wilson this thing that philosophy has never tried to do is the essence of its failure.

Wilson's account of the irrelevance of philosophy also includes the obligatory dismissal of poststructuralism/postmodernism. It's almost as if demeaning Derrida or Foucault or Francophony-ism (as Dawkins generously puts it) is a way for the science "communicator" to establish his intellectual bona fides. If you want to be taken seriously at a Tea Party get-together, you're obligated to claim that Obama is a socialist and a tyrant. And you won't get a listen in the world of Dawkins/Steven Pinker/Sam Harris/ Daniel Dennett if you can't knock the postmodernists, whoever they are. Anyway, here's what Wilson has to say:

> [Poststructuralists] doubt that the "reductionist" or "objectivist" program of brain researchers will ever succeed in explaining the core of consciousness . . . To make their argument, the mysterians (as they are sometimes called) point to the qualia—the subtle, almost inexpressible feelings we experience about sensory input.

---

* Wilson's idea of philosophy may be limited to the recent emergence of the "computational theory of mind" which argues that the brain is a computer and the mind is the software that it runs. This is not philosophy, it is an abdication to AI geeks. To say that this is the history of philosophy is to say that philosophy is about twenty-five years old. In any event, if it is the computational theory of mind that Wilson is thinking of, he should say so.

I don't mean to be unkind, but this statement is astonishingly innocent of reality. Who or what can he be thinking of? He is obviously not thinking of Jacques Derrida, although he should be. When has Derrida been called a "mysterian"? I know the sixties band called Question Mark and the Mysterians. I danced to "96 Tears" in junior high school. But my recollection is that Rudy "Question Mark" Martinez, the band's leader, said that the band was Cartesian in its philosophical orientation. (The band was originally called Epoché and the Cartesians.)

Please excuse the levity. It's a necessary antidote to this junk.

The idea that poststructuralists were ever interested in "qualia" is grotesquely wrong. David Chalmers—who looks like he could have been in a sixties rock band—and Rebecca Newberger Goldstein, a MacArthur fellow and winner of the 2014 Richard Dawkins Award, have written extensively about the qualia problem. But then they are not only philosophers but, in order, a cognitive scientist and a mathematician, and not remotely poststructural.

What Wilson ought to be discussing is Owen Flanagan's book *Science of the Mind* (1991). Flanagan criticizes "mysterians," a name he did in fact take from the sixties band. He refers to the New Mysterianism, which sounds like something that Kurt Vonnegut made up. In any case, he was using the term satirically in order to attack philosophers like Colin McGinn and . . . the aforementioned Chalmers.

This is all so confused and silly that I'm amazed that famous grown-ups created it.

These are errors that fall well within the "howler" range, and yet Wilson is not an outlier. His way of talking about philosophy is all too typical of "science communicators." They share the logic of the common conservative talk show host: if you say something often enough, it becomes true enough, or "truthy," to use Stephen Colbert's formulation. Obama is a socialist. Poststructuralists are mysterians. Wilson writes about philosophy as if he were reporting on a conversation overheard outside of a convenience mart.

Philosophy cashiered, Wilson expresses optimism that neuroscience will "solve the riddle of consciousness" and that "the solution will come relatively early." He provides a rough description of the process that could lead to this solution, most of it involving detailed neurological comparisons of "animal species that have come partway to the human level." Well and good (if you don't mind the Darwinian as-if that humans are at the apex of evolutionary progress), but it should be obvious that at best such studies will leave us with a better understanding of brain structure and not an understanding of our ability to think self-reflexively through questions like "What am I? What is an I? How should I live?" Etc.

Yet Wilson persists:

> The conscious mind is a *map* [*my emphasis*] of our awareness
> of the intersections of those parts of the continua we happen
> to occupy.

It is perfectly true that science can produce maps of the brain and that these maps can be very useful, especially for medical purposes. Beyond that, Wilson's statement is materialist dogma, and this from someone who has called scientific materialism a religion. The conscious mind is not a map, although it uses maps to negotiate the world in which it tries to function. Beyond that, "the map is not the territory."

At this point in the essay, Wilson moves beyond what an MRI scan can show, and introduces a favorite simile that he has used in many of his books: human sociobiology is like an ant colony. (Wilson is the preeminent world expert on all things ant-like.)

> The nervous system can be usefully conceived as a superbly well-organized superorganism built on a division of labor and specialization in the society of cells—around which the body plays a primarily supportive role. An analog, if you will, is to be found in a queen ant's or termite's relationship with her supporting swarm of workers. Each worker on its own is relatively stupid . . . The program directs the worker to specialize in one or two tasks at a time and to change programs in a particular sequence—typically nurse to builder or guard to forager—as it ages. All the workers together, however, are brilliant.

This is the sort of metaphor-making that TED Talks thrive on, and indeed, Wilson received a TED Prize in 2007. The scientists who present at TED confabs needn't affirm free-market capitalism directly (although many of them, like Shermer, do), so long as the *implications* of their thinking have free-market "consilience," in Wilson's terminology. In fact, TED has become a spectacularly influential force in part through its conciliation of science and libertarian economics, which it then sells to us as entertainment. And it just so happens that one of Wilson's favored ways of tarring postmodernists (again, whoever they are) is by calling them "leftists" and "socialists." Apparently, he thinks that is a bad thing.

It's true that Wilson qualifies his generalization by saying that the mind can be "usefully conceived" as an ant colony. But even if he is acknowledging that his metaphor is a metaphor, it's an especially dangerous one. Let's look at its implications. First, nature, or at least the ant part of it, is structured like an industrial society with the stupid individual worker ants given appropriately stupid functions so that the larger organism can succeed brilliantly. "Designed by geniuses to be run by idiots." Second, the human brain is organized like an ant colony; it has an infinity of parts each of which is individually useless, but together they create this brilliant thing—the human brain. Finally, the subliminal suggestion: if there is a structural analogy between ant colonies and the brain, should we be surprised if the model can be extended to other aspects of human behavior? After all, the theory of Wilson's "sociobiology" is that behavioral traits are inherited and then honed by natural selection. So no one would mistake a semiconductor factory in China for the anthills of the Florida Harvester Ant, but the original behavioral traits are similar: complex organizations run by individuals with limited tasks. A Texas Instruments factory in Chengdu is thus the evolutionary result of a trait that can also be seen in an ant colony. As Wilson writes in the introduction to his novel *Anthill*: "There are of course vast differences between ants and men. But in fundamental ways their cycles are similar. Because of it, ants are a metaphor for us, and we for them."

Once the idea that it is natural for parts to subordinate themselves to wholes is accepted, it can have profound social consequences for the human species, if not for the ants. For example, isn't the American economy structured in this way? A few years back, a metaphor similar to Wilson's was being offered by some economists as an explanation of globalization. The idea was that in a global economy there should be "head" nations where the thinking and theorizing and other brainwork got done, and then there should be "body" nations where workers would be asked to apply the elbow grease. Needless to say, in this simplistic schema the West would provide the brains and the "developing world" the brawn. Like an ant colony or the brain, no part of the global economy makes sense without the whole. More simply put, nature is organized parts, our brains are organized parts, our economy is organized parts, and it is those organizations that make you you, whether you are one of the grunts assembling clothes irons in a manufactured landscape in China, or one of a thousand brainy software developers in a Silicon Valley venture.

We're told implicitly: "Forget the touchy-feely worries of those crazy mysterian poststructuralists and their qualia or whatever it is. Our economic system, of which you are a part, just as surely as free will is a part of consciousness, *works*. It's great. The best. Science can tell you why it works. It works because it is as *natural* as ants. So you should be content doing whatever your particular organization of humans finds most appropriate for you. And be ready to switch jobs as needed. Like ant workers who can move from soldier to forager, you should be flexible. If for the first forty years of your working life you are a middle-class office manager living in Connecticut, it should not surprise you if the system needs you to make Big Macs in Galveston in your later working years. This is how nature works." In other words, *Wilson's metaphor has the tendency to naturalize gross inequality.*

Does Wilson say this explicitly? No. If you asked him about it, he would, I hope, say that this was not his intention. And he would have all sorts of plausible deniability. But I'm not concerned with blaming Wilson. What I'm concerned with is the *tendency* of science writers and libertarian economists to tell certain ideologically loaded stories that seem to rhyme. The stories become the habitual idiom in which our culture approaches every problem. The tellers of these stories party down over at TED's crib in Monterey, California, and provide intellectual cover for the brutal techno-plutocracy the rest of us have to live in.*

•

---

* The ant colony metaphor appears to be common among science explainers. In a *Scientific American* article by Daniel Dennett and Deb Roy, the authors contend that "Just as ant colonies can do things that individual ants cannot, human organizations can also transcend the abilities of individuals, giving rise to superhuman values."

Wilson has taken us from neuroscience to biology and provided two very different ways of accounting for consciousness/free will, but he's not done. In the last section of the essay, he turns to humans as storytellers, a topic he has been promoting for the last five years or so. Storytelling, it turns out, is another reason for optimism that the problem of consciousness will be solved soon.

> The final reason for optimism is the human necessity for confabulation, which offers more evidence of a material basis to consciousness. Our minds consist of storytelling.

And:

> Conscious mental life is built entirely from confabulation. It is a constant review of stories experienced in the past and competing stories invented for the future.
>
> Then he attempts to bring storytelling back into the realm of neuroscience:
>
> The stories that compose the conscious mind cannot be taken away from the mind's physical neurobiological system, which serves as script writer [*sic*], director, and cast combined.

Obviously, we're back in metaphor land, but since the topic is now storytelling, perhaps that is appropriate. Nevertheless, the lesson that Wilson draws from thinking of consciousness as storytelling will not please the mechanical materialists because it causes him to move abruptly from optimism to a kind of scientific resignation, almost a eulogy.

> The power to explain consciousness, however, will always be limited. Suppose neuroscientists somehow successfully

learned all of the processes of one person's brain in detail.
Could they then explain the mind of that individual? No,
not even close.

And this leads him to a conclusion that is, *mirabile dictu*,
strongly reminiscent of Vaihinger's *Philosophy of As-If*!

> So, does free will exist? Yes, if not in ultimate reality, then at
> least in the operational sense necessary for sanity and thereby
> for the perpetuation of the human species.

Or, as I said earlier, free will exists because "we're still using
it." But this is not why President Obama gave the Brain Activity Map Project $500 million. I know we've been told that the
essence of genius is "the ability to hold two opposed ideas in
mind at the same time and still retain the ability to function,"
but by my count Wilson is holding three mutually exclusive
ideas in one essay: neuroscience, ant analogies, and now storytelling. Do I need to say that his three reasons for optimism—
mapping neurons, sociobiology, and confabulation—cannot
possibly apply to the same thing? If they are working together,
Wilson has got some more 'splainin' to do (as Ricky Ricardo
would have put it).

Is this essay a delightful intellectual feat, a tour de force, because Wilson keeps so many balls in the air? Is it a masterpiece
of confusion? Or is it simply a mirror held up to the confusion
that reigns in science in general? As I suggested earlier, Wilson
is a juggler who finds that all his brightly colored balls have

miraculously frozen in midair. He is undecided. He is optimistically skeptical and skeptically optimistic. Oddly, in that way he is more poststructural than he knows. For Derrida, the origins of language, consciousness, free will, etc., are, after all, "undecidable."

A final word on philosophy and poststructuralism, and this time I'll do the boiling down. There is a primary philosophic idea in poststructuralism/deconstruction. It is this: deconstruction is the "critique of the metaphysics of presence." That is, it is a criticism of the idea that the objective world that our senses provide us is in fact just as it seems. Scientists who persist in believing in a reductive materialism are metaphysicians without knowing it—always the most dangerous kind of metaphysician. Deconstruction is heir to an old skepticism found in Descartes, Hume, Kant, Hegel, Nietzsche, and Heidegger. Deconstruction's contribution to this tradition is in arguing that the things we understand as real (including reified concepts like the "self") are only possible because they are "supplemented" by something that is not the thing at all, as in Jacques Lacan's famous Mirror Stage of psychological development in which the "I" (the "little man") looks into the mirror (of culture) and says, "I am *that*."

In the present case, the possibility of free will as an aspect of neuromatter is supplemented by free will as a story that we tell ourselves. *We can't look for free will in the brain without first knowing it as a narration.* So, to imagine that "free will" is a

thing is illusory; what we have in the place of the "thing" are
the stories, symbols, and social systems (judicial codes, etc.)
that employ it and thus supplement its absence. This is more or
less what Wilson is suggesting: free will exists not in itself but
in the fictions we tell about it and use in our lives.

THEY CALL HIM THE REAL PRETENDER

E. O. Wilson is a real scientist—*and* he plays one on TV and
in books.

#Buddha-Bot

THE TECHNO-BUDDHA

Most advocates for technology seem to assume that when technology moves into a traditional area of human activity it tends to make it better, medicine being the most unproblematic example. Whether that means genetic research, drug development, sophisticated diagnostic machines, neuromapping, or simply making our personal medical records instantly available to physicians, the case for medical technology is an easy one to make (even allowing for Nicholas Carr's reservations). But of course technology has moved into virtually *every* aspect of our lives—and often in ways that are not so carefully considered as they are in medicine. In recent years, the technology sector has even begun to suggest that it is the future not only of the economy, of agriculture, of medicine, and other largely empirical enterprises; it has also begun to think of itself as the future of spirituality. Usually, this doesn't mean much more than that Christianity, Judaism, and Islam should be replaced by the secular awe of scientific discovery, especially astrophysics, where one worships at the shrine of the Hubble space telescope. But then there is also the startling case of Western Buddhism, which has been transformed from a trapping of the sixties counterculture to something to be measured and put in the employ of industry.

Buddhism's presence in the West is, of course, not new. In the nineteenth and twentieth centuries, Eastern thought had a significant impact on philosophers and a powerful influence on poets. (Emerson called Thoreau the "Concord Buddha.") Arthur Schopenhauer's majestic *The World as Will and Idea*, from 1818, was the first work of philosophy to fully integrate Eastern thought—especially the *Upanishads* and Buddhism's Four Noble Truths—into its own intellectual unfolding. Hegel had a fragmentary knowledge of Hinduism and Buddhism, and Nietzsche wrote as if he had fragmentary knowledge, although by the late nineteenth century he had no excuses for not knowing it well. Both philosophers professed admiration for Buddhism's honesty, its realism, and its superiority to Christian dogma, while, in the end, finding it a philosophy of nihilism.[10] They seem to introduce Buddhism not in order to perform a good-faith investigation but in order to check it off the list of inadequate alternatives to their own thought.

More recently, Buddhism has been integrated into departments of philosophy in American universities, though most professional journals in Buddhist studies—like the *Journal of the International Association of Buddhist Studies*, or the online *Journal of Global Buddhism*—find it difficult to resist the gravitational pull of the dominant Anglo-American school broadly known as analytic philosophy, with its heavy preference for mathematics and empiricism. As *JGB* announces on its website, "The journal will function as an independent research tool itself, emphasizing surveys, the creation of databases, empirical investigations, and through the presentation of ongoing research projects."

As B. Alan Wallace writes in *Buddhism and Science: Breaking New Ground*:

> Buddhism, like science, presents itself as a body of systematic knowledge about the natural world, and it posits a wide array of testable hypotheses and theories concerning the nature of the mind and its relation to the physical environment . . . Buddhism may be better characterized as a form of empiricism rather than transcendentalism.

Wallace has used the assumption of the compatibility of Buddhism and science to create the Compassion and Attention Longitudinal Meditation (CALM) Study at the Santa Barbara Institute for Consciousness Studies. That organization describes the study in this way:

> The CALM Study will extend recent findings that training in compassion meditation reduces the types of deleterious physical and emotional responses to psychological stress that have been associated with an array of modern illnesses, including depression, cardiovascular disease, diabetes, and dementia.

In other words, Buddhism has a place in the West if it is empirical and useful.

Neuroscience has been a particularly bad actor in this regard, using fMRI technology on meditators in order to find what has been derisively called the brain's "Buddha-spot." As with neuro-science's studies of creativity, it has only been interested in gathering data (what Buddhist scholar Bernard Faure calls the "blind logic of accumulation") that it has no idea how to interpret. Its primary success has been in garnering funding for future data gathering, all with the vague and vain hope that something will be discovered that can be offered as a therapy for "our busy, stressful modern lives." The busyness and stress are apparently inevitable and not open to debate; in fact, some mindfulness therapies encourage patients to use time spent commuting to work as an opportunity for practicing mindfulness techniques. No one seems to be much interested in identifying the sources of stress and unhappiness and getting rid of them. Instead, Buddhism becomes a form of psychological triage for sorting and responding to the suffering of those in the corporate carrel, stuck in traffic, in prison, or in a war zone in the Middle East.

The best-known spokesperson for a science-based Buddhism is neuroscientist/atheist Sam Harris. As Harris wrote in a 2006 essay for *The Shambhala Sun*:

> The methodology of Buddhism, if shorn of its religious encumbrances, could be one of our greatest resources as we struggle to develop our scientific understanding of human subjectivity . . . Once we develop a scientific account of the contemplative path, it will utterly transcend its religious associations. Once such a conceptual revolution has taken place, speaking of "Buddhist" meditation will be synonymous with a failure to assimilate the changes that have occurred in our understanding of the human mind.

This tendency to make Buddhism accommodate itself to the West's empirical assumptions about the nature of reality has been a problem from the beginning. As the grand old man of Buddhist studies Edward Conze observes in the preface to his book *Thirty Years of Buddhist Studies*:

> The study of the Mahayana sutras is either left to outsiders lodged precariously on the margin of society, or is carried on for reasons which have little to do with their actual message—such as an interest in linguistic problems.

Scholars of Buddhism, he concludes, tend to take "no living interest" in their subject.

For a telling contemporary example of what Conze was concerned with, there is one of the world's leading Buddhist scholars, Richard Gombrich (former Boden Professor of Sanskrit at Oxford and author of *What the Buddha Thought*) who prefaces his public commentaries with the disclaimer "I am not a Buddhist." His interest in Western philosophy is limited to twentieth-century philosophers like Karl Popper, a philosopher of science and "critical rationalist." Gombrich's primary concern with Buddhism is the logical derivation of its ethics, and he dismisses Western Buddhism and its cult of meditation as "self-interested."

Western Buddhism's association with the sixties counterculture is being replaced not only by science but by corporations that deploy it in order to enhance their brand, promote "wellness," reduce sick days and other inefficiencies among their employ-ees, and, of course, create profitable, Buddhist-themed prod-ucts. This corporate adoption of Buddhism was made safe by science. The business world's understanding of meditation—and especially the practice of "mindfulness"—is driven not by traditional Buddhist ideas and ethics, but by neuroscience.

Take Mindfulness Based Stress Reduction (MBSR) that was developed in 1979 by Jon Kabat-Zinn, an MIT-trained sci-entist. In her cover story for the February 3, 2014, issue of *Time* magazine, Kate Pickert quotes Kabat-Zinn: "It was always my intention that mindfulness move into the mainstream. This is something that people are now finding compelling in many countries and many cultures. The reason is the science." Kabat-Zinn has played a central role in the Search Inside Yourself pro-gram developed at Google, where, their website claims, mind-fulness training builds "the core emotional intelligence skills needed for peak performance and effective leadership . . . We help professionals at all levels adapt, management teams evolve, and leaders optimize their impact and influence."

As you might suspect, there are no Buddhist sutras concerned with influence optimization or management team evolution.

And then there was the January 2014 World Economic Fo-rum in Davos where, according to Otto Scharmer (another MIT man, writing for *The Huffington Post*), corporate mind-fulness is at the "tipping point." Scharmer writes:

> Mindfulness practices like meditation are now used in tech-
> nology companies such as Google and Twitter (amongst

others), in traditional companies in the car and energy sec-
tors, in state-owned enterprises in China, and in UN organizations, governments, and the World Bank.

There is no shortage of evidence for this tipping point. General Mills makes meditation rooms available to its employees,
and Aetna CEO Mark Bertololini is committed to bringing
mindfulness benefits to all his employees. And then there are
the start-up entrepreneurs like Rohan Gunatillake's 21Awake,
manufacturer of the Buddhify app: "Modern mindfulness
wherever you are." According to Buddhify's website, it is the "#1
mindfulness app for modern life. Beautifully designed and full
of specially designed content to suit your busy city life, Buddhify
helps bring calm, concentration and compassion to whatever
you're doing and wherever you are." The app even has a feature
that—like athletic "wearables" that keep track of your running
stats—monitors your use of Buddhify in order to provide statistical measures for "how you're doing." Like an athlete in training,
you want to make sure you hit your daily meditation numbers.

Since the name of the game is stress reduction, not enlightenment, computer scientists are working on wearable monitors
to measure levels of stress. MIT's Affective Computing Center
is developing technologies to "automatically recognize stress in
order to prevent chronic psychological stress and pathophysi-
ological risks associated with it." Automatic Stress Recognition
technologies will consist of "comfortable and wearable biosen-
sors [that create] opportunities to measure stress in real-life environments . . . In this project, we modify the loss function of

Support Vector Machines to encode a person's tendency to feel more or less stressed." Perhaps if your wearable stress device starts flashing and beeping in alarm, you will be automatically signed up for a Mindfulness program in the Corporate Wellness center.

Of course, for all of their countercultural pretensions, corporations like Google, Amazon, and Apple are still corporations. They seek profits, they try to maximize their monopoly power, they externalize costs, and, of course, they exploit labor. The American technology sector has externalized the cost of industrial pollution to China's cities, where people live in a pall of smog but no one—certainly not Apple—has to bear the cost of cleanup. Apple/Foxconn's dreadful labor practices in China are common knowledge, and those Amazon packages with the sunny smile issue forth from warehouses that are more like Blake's "dark satanic mills" than they are the new employment model for the Internet Age.

The technology industry has manufactured images of the rebel hacker and hipster nerd, of products that empower individual and social change, of new ways of doing business, and now of a mindful capitalism. Whatever truth might attach to any of these, the fact is that these are impressions carefully managed to get us to keep buying products and, just as importantly, to remain confident in the goodness and usefulness of the high-tech industry. We are being told these stories in the hope that we will believe them, buy into them, and feel both hip and spiritually renewed by the association. Unhappily, in this view of things, mindfulness can be extracted from a context of Buddhist meanings, values, and purposes. Meditation and mindfulness are not part of a whole way of life but only a spiritual technology, a mental app that is the same regardless of how it is used and what it is used for. Corporate mindfulness takes something that has the capacity to be oppositional—Buddhism—and redefines it. Eventually, we forget that it ever had its own meaning.

Slavoj Žižek puts this all succinctly in his book *On Belief*:

> [Western Buddhism] enables you to fully participate in the frantic pace of the capitalist game while sustaining the perception that you are not really in it, that you are well aware how worthless this spectacle is—what really matters to you is the peace of the inner Self to which you know you can always withdraw.

In his 2012 book *The Scientific Buddha: His Short and Happy Life*, Donald S. Lopez argues that Buddhism's validity does not depend on science's confirmation of its truths, nor on its usefulness as a stress reducer. Just the opposite:

> The goal of . . . meditation . . . is stress *induction*. This stress is the result of a profound dissatisfaction with the world. Rather than seeking a sense of peaceful satisfaction with the unfolding of experience, the goal of this practice is to produce a state of mind that is highly judgmental, indeed judging this world to be like a prison.

In other words, the corporate and scientific vision of Buddhism mutes its radical potential. As Robert Aitken writes in *The*

Mind of Clover, the radical potential of Western Buddhism is in "training ourselves as a danaparamita community to become a new growth within the shell of the old society." This "new growth" is constrained by the model of corporate mindfulness.

In his tremendous book *Lack and Transcendence*, the Buddhist philosopher David Loy writes: "Buddhism does not provide a metaphysical system to account for reality but shows how to deconstruct the socially conditioned metaphysical system we know as everyday reality."

Precisely.

Unfortunately, many American Buddhists do not use it for "stress induction," as Lopez encourages. This is to some degree the case because most Western Buddhists are affluent and can go to pricey meditation retreats and buy accoutrements like Tibetan *thangkas* from the zafu store to give the right ambience to the meditation room. The Buddha Grove, an "online store dedicated to awe-inspiring Buddha statues, jewelry, meditation malas & more," provides an example of this approach. Or how about an Enso Pearl digital meditation watch ("See Time Clearly") available from Salubrion? It's an alarm clock. You don't want to get lost in the meditative haze and miss your 10:30 meeting.

The obvious peril is that consumption will win, just as it wins in the larger culture, and spiritual study and meditation will become little more than a class marker, a privilege, like belonging to a country club. In short, Buddhism becomes an acceptable occupation for what Thorstein Veblen termed the "leisure class"—another form of "conspicuous consumption."

The dissonant irony here is that the affluence that gives Western Buddhists their privilege, and gave them the opportunity to engage Buddhism in the first place, is part of what the Buddha meant by *samsara*, the world of attachment and consequent suffering. In a sense, Buddhist practice in the West is dependent upon continued delusion, especially those delusions that cause us to identify with class-appropriate roles.

A THOUGHT

To think that the mind is the consequence of neurochemistry is not necessarily a non-Buddhist thought. What's non-Buddhist is to say that chemistry makes us machines or robots. From a Buddhist perspective, the idea that we're made up of molecules ("dependent co-origination") means that the free-standing, self-contained body/ego is a delusion. It means that there is no "I." But mostly it's a way of saying that we are part of what is ("suchness"); we are taken up in the Whole. As even scientists acknowledge—after work, martini in hand: we are all ultimately stardust.

THE NEURO-INDUSTRIAL COMPLEX MAKES A HAPPY FACE

Why has corporate culture decided to get its zen on? Are business leaders just large-hearted people concerned about the welfare of their employees and willing to offer compensation beyond a salary? Or are they cynically mugging a religious philosophy only in order to enhance profit by reducing absenteeism, and to sustain customer loyalty by Buddha-branding their products?

William Davies's 2015 book *The Happiness Industry: How the Government and Big Business Sold Us Well-Being* offers a far deeper account of corporate mindfulness. In his view, what Google and others are doing is merely part of a long tradition. Part social vision and part business strategy, this tradition seeks to address the unhappiness of workers without having to change anything about itself. So meditation seminars help Google's employees manage stress without suggesting that Google itself has any role to play in the creation of said stress.

Davies acknowledges that there is a problem. Managers may now be largely free of the obligation to deal with unions, but they do have to deal with "employees who are regularly absent, unmotivated or suffering from persistent, low-level mental health problems." A large part of the reason for their psychological suffering is the unrealistic image of perfectibility that capitalism offers, in which there is "one ideal form of human existence: hardworking, happy, healthy and, above all, rich." Striving to achieve this ideal produces a society with "nothing but private fulfillment as its overarching principle." Unfortunately, for the vast majority of people, private fulfillment is a chimera. The reality is that this ideal "condemns most people to the status of failures, with only the faint hope of future victories to cling onto."

Davies contends that capitalism addresses the unhappiness of its workers by leading them to think that the source of their unhappiness is "inside themselves" (as Google would put it) and not outside in the material context in which they work. In short, capitalism tells its subjects that if they're unhappy, it's their own fault. (This has more than a passing resemblance to the more familiar claim, usually put forward by Republicans, that if you are poor it is your own fault for lacking self-discipline, for failing to get an adequate education, and for refusing hard work. Blame yourself.) And so the stressed-out software designer or the data drone with eyes crossed after a long day writing code needs to "look inside." What's outside—the character of the work itself, the company, capitalism in general—is not our concern. A worker's unhappiness may be a call for treatment, but it is not a call for critique and reform.

This theme is plenty revealing on its own, but Davies's supporting narrative about *how* capitalism succeeded in getting labor to blame itself is rich and compelling. This "blame yourself" tradition begins, according to Davies, with Jeremy Bentham and utilitarianism in the mid-nineteenth century. Bentham argued that "nature has placed mankind under the governance of two sovereign masters, pain and pleasure," much like our culture has reduced human emotions to happiness and depression. Bentham was opposed to philosophical speculation and desired to base his theory on a quantifiable basis: a science of signs of pleasure or pain. He looked to the scientific investigation of physiology to provide an index of pleasure based on things like pulse rate, but he was most interested in how money could provide a measure. Pleasurable things, he thought, would command high prices, while unpleasant things would not, making it an ideal way to measure well-being.

Davies writes:

> These were and remain the options: money or the body. Economics or physiology. Payment or diagnosis . . . When the iPhone 6 was released in September 2014, its two major innovations were quite telling: one app which monitors bodily activity, and another which can be used for in-store payments.

And so we go measuring our well-being either through surveys and data-driven happiness indexes, or through the lingering Calvinist ethos that says that money equals happiness.

Subsequent chapters trace the Benthamizing of the American lifeworld in frightening detail, modestly but regularly punctuated by the author's own "honest indignation," as William Blake put it. Davies argues that capitalism not only reduces pleasure to neurological events, but also makes it the central economic fact.

> In the early 1980s, it was discovered that dopamine is released in our brains as the "reward" for a good decision. To economists, this posed an enticing question: could value in fact be a real, chemical substance, in quantity, inside our brains? When I decide to spend £10 on a pizza, might this actually be because I will receive an *exactly equivalent* quantity of dopamine, by way of reward? . . . Perhaps it might be

possible to identify the exchange rate through which these dollar-for-dopamine trades are undertaken.

A hypothetical: once a Google employee has been educated by the neuroscientists at SIY, and once she has experienced the pleasurable, calming effects of a meditation seminar over in Corporate Wellness, she might consider attending a weekend retreat up in Mill Valley . . . depending on the cost of registration. How much money is a weekend of dopamine-rich meditative equipoise worth? $200 for sure. $500 maybe. But unless there's a celebrity guru involved, a $1,000 price tag will lead this fictional employee to take what dopamine she can get from Netflix and, naturally, pizza. She is "constantly making cost-benefit trade-offs in pursuit of [her] own interests."

Davies concludes:

> Why would anyone believe that, in our fundamental biological nature, we operate like accounting machines? The answer to that question is simple: to rescue the discipline of economics and, with it, the moral authority of money.

That's powerful stuff.

The fundamental problem that Davies confronts is not only the "neuro-industrial complex." The problem is that we live in a Money Regime. As Marx put it: "We carry our relation to others in our pocket." With Davies's guidance, we now understand that we also carry our relationship to *ourselves* in our pocket.

Many of us dislike this society of money, but we also live under the following threat: you will find a way to get money to flow through you or you will suffer. (It is the specter of homelessness that currently haunts us.) We are implicitly promised that if we accept the authority of money—if we get a STEM education, if we get a job in the information economy—we may gain access to pleasure/happiness *if we don't have a mental breakdown first.*

SEEKING MISS KITTY: A PROLOGUE

The saddest thing in the history of ideas is a noble idea so corrupted that it comes to mean the opposite of its first intended meaning. I suppose, to be charitable, this corruption can emerge from innocent stupidity, but it's difficult not to recognize how convenient the corrupted version is for the purposes of the regime du jour, especially when the original idea is dangerous or potentially destabilizing of the dominant culture.

The sentimentalizing of the Romantic metaphor of childhood as a time of intimacy with nature (as in Wordsworth's "Immortality Ode") is a good example. The innocence, the perfection, the general mindless adorability of children is one of the most enduring Romantic clichés. Its admirable origin is in work like German Romantic Philipp Runge's painting *The Hülsenbeck Children*. In this painting he intended to suggest a revolution of the spirit.

Philipp Otto
Runge, *The
Hülsenbeck
Children*, 1806

This painting is not solely concerned with the children, or
with the boy and his world-taming whip whose eyes gaze so
knowingly into our own. It is also a social and symbolic landscape. The town on the horizon, where all adult meaning has
accreted, is inert, nearly dead. But the children are warmed and
animated by the vivid sunflowers that dance above them. As
William Vaughn writes in his book *German Romantic Painting*:

> The pudgy faces and hands of the infant are alive with pri-
> mal energy, and the elder boy is shown rushing forward,
> heedlessly wielding his whip. Only the girl possesses any
> forethought. She looks back in consternation as the baby in-
> stinctively grasps at one of the lower leaves of the sunflower
> looming above him. Most arresting of all is the picture's han-
> dling of scale. Looking at the painting, we find ourselves in

the children's world. We are on their level, below the sun-
flower and close to the ground . . . The effect of all this is to
emphasize their monumental presence.

What came after the complex purposefulness of Romanticism's understanding of childhood reminds me of a scene in
Peter Sellers's early 1970s satire *The Magic Christian*, based on
a Terry Southern novel of the same name. A retired industrial-
ist named Guy Grand (Sellers) buys a "school of Rembrandt"
painting from a snooty art dealer (played by a young and already pitch-perfect John Cleese). Purchase made, Grand informs the dealer that he only wants the nose and proceeds to
cut it out with a pair of scissors. So it is with the eyes of the
Runge children; they are taken from their context, only to become the soulless void of Victorian Romantic kitsch.

Things just get worse from there. The wide, aware eyes of the Romantic child are literally emptied—a perverse confession of misappropriation—and then tied to the values of Daddy Warbucks, war profiteering, and the free enterprise system, upon which all innocence must henceforth depend. In other words, Little Orphan Annie.

You know the rest: "All jumbled up together, to compose / A Parliament of Monsters" (Wordsworth). What began as part of a revolutionary turn away from orthodox religion and toward what Wordsworth called "natural piety" becomes consumer pabulum: Margaret Keane's morose, vacant, and lemur-eyed children, or Rebecca, an American Girl doll.

And the last drooling detail:

If you have a masochistic streak, look again at the Runge painting while thinking of Hello Kitty. You'll have it right in front of you, then, the whole sorry-ass devolution.

A TALL SKINNY RICH BUDDHA

What is important to recognize, in what I have described in relation to Romantic painting, is a devolutionary tendency that has turned something that was a challenge to mainstream culture into something that is all too much like it. With Buddhism, much the same devolution was made possible by Buddhist scholars who neutered Buddhism's spirituality by recognizing it only when it could present itself empirically; by corporations who felt safe using this scientific Buddha for product branding and for workforce "wellness"; and most recently by all of us who find in Buddhism only things and identities to purchase and consume.

Perhaps the most important lesson in this history is the recognition that technology is never purely technical. Google is a technology company, but it is also the creator of narratives about what it is (scientific and yet hip, creative, and spiritual) and who we are ("moist robots," in Daniel Dennett's phrase: neuro-machines that just happen to have a Buddha-spot). What Google and its ilk have accomplished is this: they have shown that Buddhism can be used without the embarrassment of seeming soiled and hippy-like by anyone with a product to sell, high-tech or not. The prestige of science and the glamour of Google have made it possible to encase Buddhism in a package as hard and bright as a MacBook clamshell case.

So consumer Buddhism will come to look more and more like this: In March 2014, Suze Yalof Schwartz announced the opening of Unplug Meditation. Earlier in her career, Yalof Schwartz was a fashion editor at *Glamour*, *Vogue*, and *Elle*. She also ran *Tall Skinny Rich*, a website promoting the worldview of tall, skinny, rich people. ("Because everyone can look a little taller, skinnier, and richer.") Her new drop-in meditation studio is modeled after SoulCycle, the spin class "founded on the belief that fitness could be inspiring." Yalof Schwartz's drop-in meditation studios have an explicit and earnest connection to technology: "Unplug." Apparently, Yalof Schwartz is also concerned that, as Otto Scharmer puts it in his *Huffington Post* article, "our hyperconnectivity and fast-paced lives have caused us to disconnect more and more from ourselves."

So, Unplug and Google's SIY are on the same team. Nevertheless, the ironies are many: Yalof Schwartz has an anti-technology product made plausible by a program created by a technology company—Google. What's more, she has a consumer product that is anti-consumption: you can buy a pillow at Unplug that reads "Happy With Nothing" (excepting the pillow, perhaps).

In an article published on the *Fast Company* website, Ayana Byrd writes:

> Yalof Schwartz is determined to strip the "mystery" away
> that surrounds the practice and has carefully created classes

> that can get anyone on track . . . instructors offer what she describes as "an amazing dose of spirituality and science-based structure." . . . "Meditating at home is not fun for me," she says. "But meditating in a room with someone guiding me in, with music, then guiding me out . . . it feels like you did something. This isn't just meditation, it is an experience."

You might wish I were, but I'm not making any of this up.

Yalof Schwartz helps to tell many stories here, the most prominent of which is the wishful claim that there is nothing special about elite culture, not even Buddhist enlightenment. You can do it as easily as you work out with your trainer. You can be anything you want to be so long as being anything doesn't actually have a meaning. Who cares if there's any truth in her spin-class *sangha* (community) so long as you feel so much *better*. A second story would appear to be that in America there is nothing more sacred than success, and there is no better way to success than the entrepreneurial spirit, even if that spirit must first turn everything into mush, even the concept of spirit.

LIMBO LOWER NOW

Speaking of "meditating in a room with someone guiding me in and then guiding me out," the slow sex movement (playing off of the slow food movement) has recently adopted Buddha-branding in order to normalize a new practice/product called OM, or Orgasmic Meditation. Devised by charismatic founder Nicole Daedone in 2004, OM is part of a larger enterprise called One Taste and features conferences, computer apps, retreats, and coach training programs. In brief, OM is a female-focused form of meditative masturbation without the requirements of love or relationship. So, if you're a woman and you've always wanted to explore your spirituality through multiple orgasms achieved alongside a few hundred strangers, this is for you.

In addition to the rigmarole and accoutrements of Eastern spirituality, OM has its own cultish jargon. Couples begin by assuming a correct posture in a "nest" of pillows: the woman is on her back, legs butterflied, surrounded by *zafus*; a man is at her side with one leg under and one leg over her legs. (D. T. Suzuki was no more particular about the importance of posture.) The male then begins a fifteen-minute procedure by kneading the woman's thighs (this is called "grounding pressure"). The partner is asked to look at the woman's vagina and describe it (this is "noticing"). Permission ("safeporting") is then requested for genital touching. (Safeporting should not be confused with converting a person into an energy pattern through transporting. That was on *Star Trek*.)

This is all prologue to the act itself, which is, in comparison, only an old-school lubricated finger applied to the clitoris. This erotic palpation is, disappointingly, called "stroking." (One Taste has a line of oil-based lubricants called One Stroke for $15 per jar, available on their website. In case you're interested.) Finally, there is "framing," a moment in which the participants are asked to describe their feelings in the glow that follows fifteen-minute public orgasms. Said one Omer (quoted, I should add, in an article in *Playboy* called "Pleasure Seekers:

The Slow-sex Movement's Quest to Build a Better Female Orgasm"): "I felt waves of energy from my pussy up to my heart chakra and spreading around us like a lotus flower."

Call me old-fashioned, but we used to call this sort of thing a group grope. But that's just the point. OM is not about blind groping. That was all vulgar and crude, and this is enlightened and even politically correct. As Indiana University sociology professor Elizabeth Armstrong told *The New York Times*: "The notion of a San Francisco sex commune focused on female orgasm is part of a long and rich history of women being public and empowered about their sexuality."

I stand corrected.

As a business, One Taste is growing and profitable. (Can an IPO be far off?) The OMX conference in San Francisco in 2013 drew 1,000 registrants at $395 per person. On top of this, there were T-shirt sales ("The Pussy Knows"), key chains, Powered By Orgasm notepads, aluminum water bottles, shopping bags, and an iPhone app (don't use it at the local coffeehouse). Some of One Taste's business ventures are on message, like the OM introductory classes offered across the country, but others are not. OT has a site called "Orgasm Daily," which, at the moment I'm writing, is featuring blogs titled "The Joys of Insanity," "Making Love to a Witch," "How to Walk Your Beast," and "Five Ways to Electrocute Your Relationship." And for the ambitious there is a six-month mastery program that includes classes like

"How to Fuck." (There are more classes of similar subtlety, but I won't belabor the point.) This series of master classes will set the ambitious OMer back $7,500, a good-size investment, but when you're done you can set up shop in that empty storefront in the local strip mall and be on the forefront of erotic spirituality.

PORN GETS ITS CHAKRA ON

Finally, the last and what we can only hope is the lowest level of the techno-devolution of Western Buddhism, I give you the Massage Room, an Awakened Porn website:

> Samantha is relaxed and just about under the charm of George before he has started due to the way his soothing and calming energy puts each client in a totally and utterly serene state.

That's totally *and* utterly.

Massage Room doesn't really call for much in the way of analysis. It's pretty much as it appears. But the strange thing is that this all started when *neuroscience*, of all things, argued that meditation was a strictly mechanical phenomenon of the neurons. And now an only recently techno-normalized Buddhism is, in turn, helping to make various hitherto unsavory aspects of consumer culture normal. (A good throaty "That's fucked up" is called for here.) The mania for mindfulness and all things Buddhist is now a part of the normalizing and feminizing of porn (like One Taste, the Massage Room site is mostly about pleasure for the female "models" they employ). This class of

HD-quality, handsomely produced, and "female-friendly" porn is now reviewed without arched brows on websites and in magazines like *Cosmopolitan* and *Marie Claire*.

So, bizarrely, Buddhism has not only been used to rebrand technology companies (removing them from the clammy palms of the geeks and handing them over to self-styled gurus like Eckhart Tolle, a keynote speaker at Google's Wisdom 2.0), it has also helped porn on its path to transcend its sordid past and stream into the homes of the middle class via a good digital feed and an HD computer monitor. The models at Massage Room are not just sex workers, they are also—strangely!—tech workers plying their trade as Tyler Cowen's "freestylers": workers who can produce valuable commodities in tandem with "intelligent machines." (Not to mention that niche demographic that employs what are called "fucking machines," although they're not exactly intelligent. They're more like the kind of thing Dad used to invent out in his shop.)* This is something that young women across the country have discovered as they set themselves up in an obscene cottage industry made possible by bedroom webcams. They troll for paying viewers while the stuffed toys of their childhood frown in the background.

The Search Inside Yourself Institute, Unplug Meditation, One Taste, and the Massage Room—all these help those of us with "stressful modern lives" to unplug, relax, release, and "feel better about ourselves." And the techno-Buddha has helped

---

* If you have to ask, you don't want to know.

make it all possible. What any of this has done for Buddhism is another matter.

Should smiley-faced tech companies like Google be held responsible for the activities of cynical entrepreneurs like Suze Yalof Schwartz or the seamy productions of Massage Room? Probably not, even though their work has made these activities possible. But what they *are* responsible for is the removal of Buddhism from its native ethical context. Google displays itself as wealthier than the wealthy, hipper than the hippies, more creative than artists, and now wiser than the saints. All we're needed for is to provide an adoring audience and an open wallet.

COMMON KINDNESS

Buddhism, like every major world religion, believes that the primary spiritual good is to offer kindness to those who suffer and despair. For Buddhism, mindfulness, meditation, and wisdom are important, but they are refinements of the basic obligation of the spirit to be kind. You might think that the mindfulness craze would tempt a Googler or two to study the Buddha's Six Perfections. Mindfulness is a perfection, but the first two perfections are charity and compassion, and some commentators on the Perfections argue that all six are aspects of kindness. The etymology of the word "kindness" indicates that the word comes from "kind," as in "of our kind, or tribe, or nation." But Buddhist kindness is universal: treat all others (all other sentient beings) as if they were your own mother. Yet on the whole, geek meditators are more interested in getting "happy" than in coming to terms with kindness, mom be damned.

But it is not necessary to be a born-again Buddhist to understand something about our need for kindness. For example, somewhere in that ocean of acute perception that we know as *In Search of Lost Time*, Marcel Proust makes the following observation: the most common thing about humans is not common sense but human kindness. Unhappily, he goes on, our natural disposition to kindness is too often defeated by our contrary disposition to self-interest. Buddhist dharma puts much the same dynamic in these terms: everyone shares in Buddha-nature, but that can be lost through anger, greed, and delusion. As a result, there is suffering.

This is something that has been observed time and again about Americans. We're a nice people, a generous people, a *kind* people. And yet the policies of our government are cruel and nakedly self-interested. In 1976, I was teaching at the University of Iowa when an exiled member of the administration of Salvador Allende asked if he could speak to my class about what had happened in Chile with the CIA-sponsored overthrow of Allende's government and the murder of thousands of students and leftists. He said to my class, "You know, traveling in your country, a person cannot help but be impressed by your kindness. But you do not understand how cruel your government is. You do not understand what you do to the rest of the world when you elect these 'representatives.'" The Republican fury over Affordable Health Care, President Obama's executive actions protecting immigrant families, and the establishment of diplomatic relations with Cuba, are but the most recent examples of our de facto cruelty. Say what you like about the shortcomings of the Obama presidency—all these actions, insufficient though they may be, begin in compassion for the suffering of large groups of disenfranchised people. Yes, this compassion will be handed over to the compassion bureaucracy, a sort of "systems morality" whose version of kindness is usually muted by paperwork; nevertheless, the ghostly trace of kindness hovers in the background.

Proust advocated generosity and kindness before all else. But his native generosity became the acid of social criticism when his unflinching, unapologetic regard fell upon the cruelty of self-interest. He considered cruelty more than anything else just maddeningly, puzzlingly, and infinitely *stupid*. The stupidity of class arrogance. The stupidity of anti-Semitism. The stupidity of homophobia. Time and again, he discovered the self-interested desire to be an aristocrat, to have wealth, or simply to get laid at the root of the most unspeakable cruelty.* For the gentle Marcel, deliberate unkindness, especially when

---

* The scene in *In Search of Lost Time* in which the "invert" (homosexual) Baron Charlus is cruelly humiliated by his ex-lover is painful to read. Charlus is himself an exploitive, hedonistic, and self-absorbed character. Proust's point would seem to be that even when directed at the worst people, cruelty is a perversion of common kindness.

motivated by self-interest, hurt him and angered him more than anything else he could name.

But I think we need to add something to Proust's intelligent observation. We need to add the further irony that we are wrong to think that cruelty functions in our self-interest. Cruelty does not work. In both the short and long run, cruel efforts to maintain self-interest have the consequence of *making us conspire against ourselves*. By acting cruelly in our self-interest, we actually become conspirators in our own defeat.

You might call this the law of karmic return. The CIA calls it blowback and figures it into the cost of doing business. I think it is more insidious than that. We conspire against ourselves in all sorts of ways, most of which are so familiar that they seem almost like common sense. The root problem is that all our decisions go into a rational machinery, the algorithms through which "intelligent machines" conduct the social calculus of "benefit." Thus, the infamous "cost-benefit analysis." So we think, "If I clear-cut this forest I can sell the timber and plant soybeans for export to China, a very profitable move. But if I cut down the forest we may not have air to breathe or a stable climate in the future. Animals will be deprived of habitat. Species may go extinct. Oh, fuck it, why should my forest be responsible for the future when it can be profitable now?"

This is not the exclusive logic of corporate capitalists. It was also the logic of Brazil's left-wing government when it was led by Luiz Inácio Lula da Silva. Brazil's deforestation of the Amazon increased by 40 percent under da Silva's watch in 2003 alone. "The Amazon is not untouchable," said da Silva. This, obviously, placed the burden of feeding the poor squarely on the backs of parrots and leopards.*

Meanwhile, Brazilian agribusiness kings like Blairo Maggi made conflict of interest a virtual requirement for governance. Not only was Maggi owner of one of the largest soybean production and export companies in Brazil, he was also the governor of the state of Mato Grasso ("dense jungle"). The Amazon will soon be just another fantastical postmodern location, so familiar to North Americans, where the names of places no longer have any relationship to what's actually in the place. Mato Grasso will refer to a place that is no more than a factory for exchange value in a soybean mono-culture, just as Illinois is a "prairie state" with a mere 0.1 percent of its original prairie remaining. Of course, once the original plant/animal/human inhabitants are gone, we wax sentimental. The things we slaughter become our heritage.

The jungle or the prairie, parrots or bobolinks—none of them ever has the opportunity to argue its own value as *being*, as things that deserve respect simply because they are. This reveals a grave spiritual flaw in their masters: the governors, developers, and agribusiness kings of the world. The ruling order has no moral right to rule because it makes its daily purpose the defeat of the future. The accountant's logic that concludes that

---

* This continues: after fifteen years of steadily reducing the rate of deforestation, President Dilma Rousseff appointed Katia Abreu—also known as "Miss Deforestation" and the "Chainsaw Queen"—as her agriculture minister.

our "interest" is in "profit" assures a future defined by cruelty, but in the long run it will be understood as self-defeat.

National self-interest is thus indistinguishable from global legalized violence aimed at humans, the natural world, and ultimately being itself, before which our captains of state stand with all the wonder of a gourmand before a steak. They're going to eat it up.

#Eco-Bot

WELCOME TO MY WORLD-BOT

At present, environmentalism is not so much a set of values as it is a menu of strategies for compromising those values (assuming they're remembered at all). Honestly, what values ground any form of cap-and-trade? What values ground our commitment to the idea that global warming will be solved if we can reduce atmospheric carbon dioxide to 350ppm? Environmentalism is about deal making in a moral abyss. The advantage in this is that because its concessions have taken the place of its values, it is able on occasion to declare victory and walk away from the wreck.

Environmentalism's greatest victory in recent years is that it has gained near universal recognition for the concept of sustainability. But what exactly is sustainability? Sustainability is, of course, the Good. That "of course" is our first clue that what we are really talking about is a very successful piece of ideology. When "sustainability" is invoked—as it is persistently invoked by environmentalists, the media, politicians, and corporations—we are expected to *bow down*. Rare is the person who dares to speak against it. (Tea Party conservatives duly noted and excepted.) Nevertheless, sustainability's claim to being the Good is a lie. What it is, in fact, is the most recent example of moral shuffling in the West's efforts to confront the problem of our "relationship to nature." The idea that we should be one with nature is rarely allowed more than a brief mention. How has this come about?

In the late nineteenth century, beginning with the national parks and conservation movements, the problem of nature was taken from the Romantics, the Transcendentalists, and the self-made mystics (like our own John Muir) and put in the hands of the biologist. We began thinking of nature as a complex system. An ecosystem. It was this movement from nature philosophy to science-based ecology that made the idea of sustainability possible. Even the saintly Aldo Leopold made a contribution to this. He was a scientist first and foremost, interested in describing natural systems. Leopold's way of thinking about the natural world was in the end mechanistic. He wrote, "To keep every cog and wheel is the first precaution of intelligent tinkering." He thought of nature as a "biotic mechanism." Walt Whitman he was not.

Of course, it is not Leopold's science that his readers admire in him; it is his loving attention to the details of the natural world. In this he *was* Whitmanesque. Ironically, it is exactly this "loving attention" that ecological science is incapable of accounting for. The philosophical and spiritual poverty of ecology comes to this: *its empirical realism cannot explain how we humans can be sufficiently independent of nature in order to love it*. Ecology cannot account for "care." Is the caring gaze that observes how the "rough legged hawk . . . drops like a feathered bomb into the marsh" also a part of a "biotic mechanism"? Is Aldo Leopold's "attention" a feat of biological engineering? If not, then we obviously need something beyond science-based ecology to account for it. Because, in the end, it is exactly our loving awareness of the natural world that is the point. This awareness does not stand at a distance from the hawk; it is self-consciousness of the whole: man, nature, and the cosmos as one.

Leopold described the human urge to economic development as a kind of dying from its own "too-much." Were Leopold here today I think he would have to be told that we are presently dying from the too-much of science and technology, the too-much of ecology, and certainly the too-much of sustainability. For what science allows in the concept of sustainability is this: nature's system can be integrated with the system of corporate industry. That's the story and the ideology of sustainability. Sustainability is an effort to integrate ecological thinking with the very industrial practices that put nature in peril in the first place. No longer is industry a "dark satanic mill." Rather, it is a perverse utopia of the forest and the factory as one. Henceforth, we're told, it's going to be a green collar world. As a recent television advertisement explained it: Where is a perfect world of clean water and air, no landfills, and 100 percent recycling? A Subaru plant in Indiana! Even better, according to Living PlanIT: in the future, cities will not only be "green," they will themselves be ecosystems of industry, commerce, residence, and open green space. If a manatee floundering in petroleum begs to differ, well, let him! But the courts will find that aquatic mammals "lack standing."

With all this in mind, it is clear why it might be tempting for environmentalism to declare victory and walk away. Take, for instance, Ken Burns's 2009 film *The National Parks: America's Best Idea*. Our national parks are surely one of the earliest examples of the logic of sustainability, balancing the need for wild spaces against the need for what we delicately call "resource extraction." Accordingly, the film celebrates our national parks and encourages us to do the same. The film also claims to be about an "idea," although it never becomes clear just what kind of "idea" a national park represents. The "best." Okay. But the film itself is largely the presentation of a series of historical "facts," rather than ideas.

In fact, Burns's film seems mostly blind to any ideas that might move among these facts. At times, he seems perversely determined not to understand what he himself has put directly before us. This refusal creates many cringe-worthy moments. One moment the viewer is moving effortlessly forward, gently propelled by Burns's fluid technique of panning across still photographs, Peter Coyote's soothing and sincere narration in the background, when suddenly . . . the Great Cringe. If it were a book, you'd throw it across the room.

The most grotesque of these cringe-worthy moments is the introduction of John D. Rockefeller, Jr., as one of the great philanthropic heroes in the establishment of our national parks. In 1928, Rockefeller stepped forward with $5 million to save the Smoky Mountains. He thus put, the film blandly asserts, a "great family fortune" to public use. What isn't said— and it is almost incredible that it needs to be pointed out—is that Rockefeller's fortune came from his father's founding of the Standard Oil Trust, notorious for its cut-throat business practices, for its use of Pinkerton goons, and for enforcing hideously exploitative wages and murderous conditions for workers in its mining operations. (It was at a Rockefeller mine that the IWW's Frank Little was murdered by company thugs in 1917.) The Rockefeller mine in Butte, Montana, turned that town into what it is to this day: one of the most toxic spots on the face of the earth. (Dashiell Hammett called it "Poisonville" in his novel *Red Harvest*.) The mine (Anaconda Copper) created mountains of toxic slag, polluted 130 miles of the Silver Bow Creek (known to locals as Shit Creek for its sulphurous stench), and filled an open pit with billions of gallons of acidic water. The mine remains a giant crypt for the thousands of workers who lost their lives underground and whose bodies were never found. When the mines became unprofitable, Rockefeller simply abandoned the town and pulled out. (The site is presently the responsibility of, appropriately, British Petroleum.)

John D. Rockefeller, Jr., continued his father's methods for profit extraction, including the pitiless oppression of miners, culminating in the Ludlow Mining Massacre of 1914. After the massacre, Rockefeller testified before Congress defending his company and arguing for the need for "open" shops.

> ROCKEFELLER: There is just one thing that can be done to settle this strike, and that is to unionize the camps, and our interest in labor is so profound and we believe so sincerely that that interest demands that the camps shall be open camps, that we expect to stand by the officers [who had been shooting at the miners] at any cost.

> CONGRESSMAN: And you will do that if it costs all your property and kills all your employees?

> ROCKEFELLER: It is a great principle.

Rockefeller paid for the Smoky Mountains National Park with the blood of miners, a fact that shouldn't be lost on a part of the country synonymous with mining. To say that he may have taken from the public but his philanthropy also gave back—provided it with a national "playground"—is brutal paternalism.* It is the same paternalism that argued to the miners at Ludlow that they had no cause for unionizing, let alone revolting, because the company had provided them with housing and a store, and all they had to worry themselves with was working. (Hi-Ho! Hi-Ho!)

Our contemporary philanthropists might say, "Sure it's

---

* The billionaires of the present are fine-tuning philanthropic paternalism. The only gift they're giving is to themselves. Barry Diller, the media mogul, is spending $130 million on a new park on an island in the Hudson River and just a short walk from his office in Chelsea.

blood money, but now you have the great gift of Yellowstone."
As if Yellowstone, or Yosemite, or the Tetons were things that
could be given to us by the representatives of wealth, and that
we should be grateful for a gift that is really little more than a
strategic forbearance from sacking these places as they did the
Hetch Hetchy Valley or that little patch of prairie down the
road from you.

You have to wonder about Burns's role in all this. Is it pure
cynicism? Has he bowed to pressure from PBS, which would
like—thanks a lot—to continue getting grants from Rockefeller, or David Koch, or the Cato Institute, or any one of
a number of ultra-conservative individuals and organizations
that seem ever more in control at PBS?[13] Whatever the reason,
from this point forward *The National Parks* is a film without a
conscience.

Perhaps *The National Parks* provides images of the beauty
and even the spirituality of nature. The film is accompanied (as
always with Burns) by spectral pianos tinkling in the distance,
which well up symphonically in the course of the film, leaving
its viewers with a feeling of national pride, aesthetic joy, and a
sense that something magnificent has been accomplished. But
at this moment the film is pure ideology. Nowhere does it dare
to suggest that the National Park system is also our *worst* idea
because it puts a boundary on nature beyond which we are free
to be as destructive as we like. Drive back across a park boundary and suddenly you're in Petroleum World ("our national automobile slum," as James Howard Kunstler put it).

Of course, people like Burns would like you to think that what's outside the park is the city and its highways, which are not to be confused with nature. The city is a very different matter altogether, and none of nature's business. In the near future, climate change will show us the true limits of this dualistic assumption. Global warming presents the greatest physical and intellectual challenge to sustainability's ability to balance and separate nature and industry. In the age of climate change, the boundary between nature and civilization means nothing. The pine bark beetle that presently ravages forests ever farther to the north was not consulted about these boundaries. ("You can't eat that forest, it's a National Park!") And that's just a small part of the devastation that will be brought by global warming.

Soon the moral shuffling of sustainability, of tinkering with "parts per million," will be forced to make a much, much greater wager when scientists and technicians are asked to engineer not only national parks and automobile factories but also the enormity of what they call the "biosphere," a word that begs the question: if you think you live in something called a biosphere, you already think of it as an engineering problem.

Our situation is worthy of Greek tragedy because we have an alternative, but like the old men who cannot heed Cassandra's warnings, we seem fated not to remember or understand it. We have an understanding of Nature that is philosophically, aesthetically, and spiritually derived, and it has been available to us for more than two centuries. Through this version of

Nature we have understood that we are not separate from it. Nature is not something that stands opposite our analytic gaze. It does not require engineering. It doesn't ask anything of us, and yet it does not exist without us.

It comes to this: Nature is what we are—*when we are most worthy of ourselves.*

For an engineer, that is a nonsensical thing to say. An engineer would prefer that we speak of ecosystems and biospheres. Ironically, by thinking of nature in this way we have made it clear that nature is all too literally a reflection of what we are: if we are nothing but mechanical materialists, then nature will be a machine and heir to all the ills of machines (especially entropy, aka pollution). We are witnesses to that. Soon we will witness even greater follies as scientists attempt to provide last-ditch solutions for global warming (geo-engineering) by employing "stratospheric sulphate aerosols" and similar schemes.

As Louis Armstrong sang: "What a wonderful World-Bot."

OUR ULTIMATE CONCERNS

The greatest moral problem for the concept of sustainability is that it doesn't have what the theologian Paul Tillich called an "ultimate concern." Environmentalism has finite concerns, like mercury levels in fish or parts-per-million of greenhouse gases, but it has no ultimate concerns. To have an ultimate concern would mean that environmentalism would have to finally become a thing that could commit itself to an ideal and know exactly what it meant by that commitment.

If environmental philanthropy were to discover its own sense of moral purpose, it would find itself in a challenging new context. To cut a deal in keeping with the "best practices" of a bureaucracy is one thing, but to cut a deal that violates our own ultimate concerns is quite another. For Tillich, sin is whatever separates us from our ultimate concerns. But "no worries," as we say these days, corporate sustainability is there to make sure all our decisions are pragmatic in the most vulgar sense: they put off the final day when all our moral shuffling comes to a conclusion.

ETHICAL OIL

In Canada, Prime Minster Harper forbids the use of the term "tar sands" for the bituminous muck that is being cooked out from under Alberta—lovely We-Got-Oil-Bitch Alberta, as they write on their T-shirts. If you want to stay in good odor with the central government, you'll say "oil sands." And you'll listen to Mr. Harper when he explains—with a logical grimace revealing that an idea can be both stupid and victorious—that the oil sands are "ethical oil" because Canadians are well known for being nicer than Arabs.

Ya, you betcha!

Meanwhile, our northern neighbors have exited the Kyoto climate agreement, and quite rightly, too: Canada's production of greenhouse gases has sent it soaring beyond its original commitments like a smoggy *pas d'élévation*.

Ethical oil! This new self-valuation surely feels to Mr. Harper like divine grace, some sort of flowing down of radiance from on high. But it seems to me more like the logic of a bug, of the pine beetle, perhaps, which—thanks to global warming—is free at last from Canada's murderous winters. It is chewing its way through the Boreal forests eating everything that gets in its way, leaving nothing for the comfort of its old age. Beware, Mr. Harper, it's Quebec or bust for these bugs. Soon, they'll be gnawing at the legs of your desk and filling the cuffs of your linen slacks with sawdust.

DESIGNATED SUFFERING

Commentators, journalists, and, on exceptionally clear days, their audiences are now beginning to wonder why it is that with fatal environmental problems bearing down upon us, with global warming threatening agriculture and our minimal ability to feed ourselves, the rich and powerful aren't more actively attempting to remedy the situation. Worse, why do they so often seem to want to do just the opposite of what is required?

This question is easy to answer if we understand the psychology of the capitalist. Easy and disturbing. The logic of capitalism acknowledges that there will be destructive consequences for its activities. Economists even have a name for it: negative externality. This is also known as "externalizing cost" when it comes time for somebody other than the perpetrator to pay for the damage. It is a secular form of what the generals call "collateral damage," which means that the wrong person got blown up. Or, as one might say, "We didn't mean to pollute that river with coal ash. We were only pursuing private prosperity and personal happiness. In the meantime, we're glad to have someone else pay to fix it." But what do you do when it's not a river—when it's a whole world that has been trashed? Are taxpayers going to have to pay for a new planet?

So the oligarchs and their minions, the so-called 1 percent, aren't missing anything. They're not stupid. If they choose to do nothing about looming global catastrophe, it is because they don't want to do anything. And they do not want to do anything because the threat of destruction is, frankly, not persuasive to them. Those who benefit from capitalism understand that it has always depended on suffering, and they have confidence that if someone is to suffer it won't be them. "Let the songbirds suffer in my place," they say. "Or those fucking—what do they call 'em—manatees. There's only about ten of them left anyway. And, we admit, the miscellaneous poor will suffer, here and in those faraway countries, but why shouldn't they suffer? Look at them! They're rather good at it. Besides, the humans could use a little downsizing."

Pereat mundus, dum ego salvus sim!*

This insight is the key to understanding Congressman Paul

---

* Let the world perish so long as I am safe.

Ryan's 2014 Republican budget proposal. It radically cut all social welfare, especially for food and health care for the poor. Ryan's budget had the virtue of making it clear who the designated sufferers were to be, and in recent years that designation has been appropriate to an ever-widening population.

The rich aren't missing anything. They get it. It's we who are clueless when we operate under the liberal delusion that no one should have to suffer, that we're all in this thing together, and once a danger is understood we'll take steps to protect our fellow citizens, we'll all pull together, politics stop at the shoreline, and all that palaver.

It is President Obama who is obtuse when he says of the critics of his health plan: "I have to admit, I don't get it. Why are folks working so hard for people not to have health insurance?" Folks? The grotesque social inequalities Obama talks so much about have a psychological reality. Anyone can see that we are not one. Not even close. The Republican Party understands and accepts this; they are not "folks." They imagine themselves to be the winners, and they mean to keep it that way.

For those who will thrive in spite of climate disaster, the future will not be apocalyptic; in fact, it promises to be charming and magical. While "folks" worry about drought, flood, fire, food shortages, bankruptcy over medical bills, and, let's not forget, zombies, their betters can look forward to the coming marvel of virtual money, e.money, digital currency, and Bitcoins galore. Disaster? They're swimming in virtual wealth! Fill the freaking swimming pool with it and download escort girls from Night Candy to jump in! Soon they will be able to strap on Oculus Virtual Reality goggles, enter a Bloomingdale's simulacrum and lift wonders from the shelves while a silently grinding device in their purse or on their hip does the math on their purchases. And then in some far-off misty place—the "Cloud," as they say—calculations and small deductions will be made (unless Russian hackers get there first and turn the digits into Mercedes and swank Black Sea dachas). Finally, for their shopping convenience, Amazon will have their loot air-dropped by a delivery drone.

I suppose the Mexican landscapers will have to start wearing hard hats.

Should someone ask why these privileged shoppers should be allowed to thrive while the planet burns, they will simply turn on their smartphones and open their electronic wallets. See? A thousand, a million, a billion, a godzillian. Now do you get it? As Chico Marx said in *The Cocoanuts*, "I gotta lotsa numbers."

Wealth will be under no obligation to make sense in relation to the impoverished and frightening hordes swarming in the dystopic hinterlands, the parched central valleys where lettuce once grew. The e.bucks and other virtual currencies will have no objective value, not in gold, not in collateral, and certainly not in the fiduciary authority, the good faith and credit of the nation state, which is now a bit player (if you'll excuse a pun). But, then, virtual money is nothing new. Money has always been virtual, a fantasy legitimating the relationship between power and misery. At least in the age of Bitcoin the Money-Bot stands naked, confessing that its only reality is the pure abstraction of force and privilege.

Charles Darwin believed that with natural selection, "all corporeal and mental endowments will tend to progress towards perfection." But can the modern oligarch be what evolution has been progressing toward for the last two million years? Are these self-destructive and vainglorious creatures really the "fittest"? The most dominant members of the most dominant species in the long history of life on earth behaving like a perverse crow that gathers into its nest a treasure of shiny bottle caps, shreds of aluminum foil, a glass earring... and then shits on it? If this is so, then evolution may be a scientific fact, but it is a very bad idea.

NATURE'S CITY

When we think about the city, our problem is that we think we already know what it is. We think this because we have been repeatedly told the same tales about it, all coming from the usual suspects: planners, engineers, politicians, Chamber of Commerce honchos, and Silicon Valley know-it-alls.

We are told that the city is the opposite of nature—you know, city mouse and country mouse, factories and national parks, skyscrapers and camping under the stars—in spite of the fact that we tend to engineer both. We think that the city has mostly to do with its buildings, roads, and systems of water, power, and sewage. The city is its infrastructure. The city is the business of experts, city planners, and engineers, of which every city council has an army. They're a bureaucratic lot and use the jargon that has mesmerized planning committees for the last two decades: they identify stakeholders, draw up strategic plans, implement, monitor, manage outcomes, and seek the holy grail of planners: "best practices." While planners talk about the "sound analysis of available information emphasizing stakeholder participation," all you want to ask is, "Why are we living like this? I don't think I want to live like this. And I really don't want to have to talk like this. Stakeholders!" These technocrats believe that the city's problems can be solved if we're more rational, more efficient, and more conscious of the consequences of our decisions. They seek the perfect structural arrangement of things, as if a city were simply a mechanical problem. But this is to think, as Hegel wrote of phrenology, that the city's reality is a "bone."

But there are worse things than a bone—a virtual bone, for example, something even a dog won't go for. Why trust our city to mechanical engineers when we can hand it over to people who learned their trade playing *SimCity*? We'll all feel smarter, more creative, hipper, and way more prosperous with Silicon Valley's boy geniuses in charge. I speak now of the "charter city," precocious heir to special "enterprise zones," charter schools, privatized prisons, and other profitable enterprises carved out of public space, where tax concessions and reduced regulations are the norm.

One of the leaders of the charter city movement is Paul Romer, a University of Chicago physicist turned "new-growth"

economist. In a TED Talk he delivered in 2009, Romer described charter cities in this way:

> So the proposal is that we conceive of something called a
> charter city. We start with a charter that specifies all the rules
> required to attract the people who we'll need to build the
> city. We'll need to attract the investors who will build out
> the infrastructure—the power system, the roads, the port,
> the airport, the buildings. You'll need to attract firms, who
> will come hire the people who move there first. And you'll
> need to attract families, the residents who will come and live
> there permanently, raise their children, get an education for
> their children, and get their first job.
>
> With that charter, people will move there. The city can
> be built. And we can scale this model. We can go do it over
> and over again.

Or there is LivingPlanIT's "Urban Operating System"
(UOS), directed by former Microsoft executive Steve Lewis.
In brief, UOS is an operating system for a city, just as your
computer has an operating system. But Lewis is just as likely
to refer to it as an eco-system (thus planIT/planet; get it?). As
their website puts it:

> LivingPlanIT is focused on delivering a platform which ac-
> celerates and optimizes the delivery of Future Cities. De-
> ployed in association with an extensive multi-sector partner
> ecosystem, developers, building owners, and service pro-
> viders use this platform to envisage, design, manufacture,
> assemble, operate, service, maintain, and decommission
> buildings more efficiently, improving performance in terms
> of environmental, economic, and social sustainability.

That's a lot of verbs and verbiage, but I can see the appeal. Want to live in a city, start a business? Just plug in. This is in all likelihood the sort of city that Tyler Cowen's denizens of Tiny Town will live in. With its free municipal WiFi, even the poor will live on the cutting edge. But there are skeptics. As Ava Kofman writes for *Jacobin*:

> As top-down city design becomes a market commodity, we will soon be forced to choose between the urban operating systems we want to inhabit. The choice might even be made for us through competition and mergers. In Songdo [China], Cisco is installing its TelePresence technology in every apartment, under the assumption that if you integrate it everywhere, people will inevitably live with it.

And that will be fine except that what people will plug into will have no history and no social traditions that are its own. But who needs traditions when you can download apps?

While some of these charter city plans seem farfetched, the fact is that they are presently under construction and visible to all in New York in the form of ex-Mayor Michael Bloomberg's ambitious Hudson Yards project. As William Davies writes in *The Happiness Industry*:

> The Hudson Yards real estate project on the West Side of Manhattan is the largest development in New York City since the Rockefeller Center was built in the 1930s. When completed, it will be home to sixteen new skyscrapers, containing office space, around 5,000 apartments, retail space and a school. And thanks to a collaboration between city authorities and New York University (NYU), initially brokered

by former mayor Michael Bloomberg, it will also be one vast
psychology lab. Hudson Yards will be one of the most ambitious examples of what the NYU research team term a
"quantified community," in which the entire fabric of the
development will be used to mine data to be analysed by
academics and businesses.

It should be observed that charter cities are not entirely new,
although the idea that they might be run through operating systems would certainly seem to be. In fact, I grew up in a nine-
hundred-square-foot stucco cottage in a "vet-village" suburb to
San Francisco, San Lorenzo, California—Levittown West, as it
was known—a city whose only tradition was that there was once
a fruit stand owned by a Filipino man on Camino Viejo. (San
Lorenzo's developers were not sentimental about history and did
not think it important to preserve either fruit stand or *camino*,
the last *cosa vieja* [old thing] in our town, excepting an old cem-
etery with its equally implausible evocations of death and the
past.) San Lorenzo Village was one of the first "planned communities," with parcels designated for schools, churches, parks, and
retail centers. The little homes were precut and then assembled
on site. This "California method," as it was called, was different
from what is now envisaged for the charter city, in that the developers eventually went away and the homeowners got to run their
little "village." But for the charter city, software is forever.

Beyond the technocratic hubris, what is most disturbing
about the planned communities of the 1950s and the charter cities of tomorrow is the notorious soullessness of these
places. Criticism of this soullessness has been mostly left to

musicians, beginning with Malvina Reynolds's folk song "Little Boxes" and Frank Zappa's "Plastic People" and continuing through Radiohead's "Fake Plastic Trees" and Arcade Fire's "Sprawl I (Flatland)." The manufactured hometown is a "town full of rubber plans."

Fine places if you're a robot, but if not, not.

In spite of this, there are still some people—acting as if they were in a Frank Capra movie turned vastly cynical—who continue to speak of something other than the techno-engineer's city-as-(virtual)-bone. They claim that the city is its spirit—its civic spirit, as civic leaders say when lighting the town hall Christmas tree. This trite, pre-digested language, the lingua franca of every hometown newspaper, creates the magical capacity to talk about things that haven't existed since Levittown was rolled off assembly lines for returning veterans of World War II. The idea that there is a spirit that animates and unites residents of our cities is an insult to whatever is left of native American intelligence. If we look out over the five-lane horror of big city commuting, a city beltway lined with franchise strip malls and subdivisions, the word "spirit" is something for choking on.

All of which is a way of saying that the first problem in thinking about the city is penetrating beneath all the received ideas that we have about it. All that expert thoughtlessness and all those clichés that would like to do our thinking for us. So let us ask: What is a city?

Once we've asked that question, we quickly come to the point where we have to admit (to paraphrase St. Augustine), "I know what a city is until I think about it." Even to say, as virtually every mainstream historian of the city does, that the city is the "defining artifact of civilization" is deeply misleading because it assumes the existence of a continuity between ancient, medieval, and modern cities. (It is also a stupefying tautology.)

But the modern city, especially the American city, has almost nothing to do with anything prior to 1850. It is certainly not a Greek city, a polis. The Greek polis, Athens in particular, was not simply its center, its architectural monuments, or its market, the *agora*. It was also the plains surrounding the city. To be a citizen was to have an identity not just with the temple and the markets of the center, but also with the farms, the olive groves, vineyards, and pastures of the countryside. A peasant in the farthest corner of Attica was still called an Athenian. By contrast, here in Illinois, Chicago treats its agricultural "downstate" as both an object of derision and a sort of domestic Third World whose tragedies and poverty one observes with a distant disinterest.

Our experience of the city doesn't have much to do with the great European cities of the nineteenth century either. When we read of them in Tolstoy, Balzac, Proust, or Edith Wharton, it seems as if they are eternal things that must still be with us. But the truth is that as late as the mid-1870s there were only four European cities with a population of over one million (London, Paris, Berlin, and Vienna). To be a city of 200,000 was to be a major population center. Los Angeles alone now dwarves *all* of those populations together. The physical footprint of the great cities of Europe in the nineteenth century was almost medieval in comparison with today's megalopolis. With the exception of industrial London, the European cities of the period were an expression of an imperial culture that is (blessedly) foreign to us now. The last person to think of the city in this way was Hitler, with his little detailed models of the monuments, theaters, and museums he would build in his hometown of Linz.

More than anything else, the city as we know it is the result of human migration beginning in the second half of the nineteenth century, continuing beyond World War II, and, unbelievable though it seems, further intensifying in the present. Tens of millions of Europeans came to the United States between 1850 and 1915, the vast majority of them from the countryside. But here, for the most part, they located in cities. There was enormous domestic migration as well, as families left the countryside for employment in urban areas. This was so even as late as the 1940s and '50s.

In my own case, both of my parents were children of farm families from the Northern Plains and the Northwest, but they lived their married lives in the San Francisco area. I mention these personal details because the growth of the American city is not an abstraction, it is something people have lived. Of course, we've always been told that people moved in order to pursue "opportunity," but the truth is, obviously, that they had little choice, as the ongoing abandonment of our rural towns testifies.

The city was not a destination for the last 150 years because people thought it would be nice to live in town, where they might enjoy our fabled coffee drinks and shopping emporiums. The city has been and remains an expression of capitalism, and its virtues are bourgeois: efficiency, specialization, and standardization. As British historian Eric Hobsbawm relates in *The Age of Capital*, the first English that the International Harvester Company taught its Polish workers in 1870 was: "I hear the whistle. I must hurry." America, he concludes, "was not a society but a means of making money." The American city was not unlike the first great products of American industrialism itself: the Colt revolver and the Winchester rifle. Gun manufacturing taught American industry about mass production, standardization, and the virtues of interchangeable parts, and the American city that industrialism produced was itself a very big gun: standardized, hugely profitable, and morally indifferent about any victims.

This is the city of the last 150 years deprived of its illusions. The charming sobriquets that we give our cities—the Big Apple, City of Angels, Baghdad-by-the-Bay, Windy City—are nothing more than picture-book thinking for the benefit of tourists and the child-minded. The terse reality is that the city as we know it and live it is a profit scheme, and a future dominated by charter cities built on digital operating systems created by giant corporations will only make the scheme more insulting and inexorable. The charter city is not a home; it is a corporate mandate.

The charter city is the conclusion of a process that was begun with the pitiless destruction of city centers across the country by General Motors, Standard Oil and Firestone in the 1930s and '40s. They bought tram and interurban rail lines in city after city, tore them up, and created the great suburban principle: get in your car or stay home. Los Angeles was their most notorious victim, but even midsize cities became mini-L.A.s with massive beltways around which hapless residents sped as if they were in a particle collider. This destruction is no longer limited to the city center but stretches out for thousands of square miles in the Great American Automobile Desert.

The world that GM built is the tragic conclusion of what Freud called the "Prosthetic God," the ultimate degree of human power amplified by machines. As Freud wrote in *Civilization and Its Discontents*: "Man has, as it were, become a kind of prosthetic God. When he puts on all his auxiliary organs he is truly magnificent." In the era of global warming, we should add that he is also truly doomed.

For capitalism, then, the city is only a function in the great megalopolitan discovery that there is profit in congestion, whether that means captive markets and populations of surplus labor, or a city OS serving as the underlying platform for the Internet of Things. During economic booms, parts of the human population may rise, find employment, and enjoy higher wages, but during a bust they once again sink down into that massive "surplus" of the unemployed, the miscellaneous poor.

The real story of the most recent recession was not the evaporation of trillions of dollars of wealth but the emergence of a vast social insecurity that was shocking to those who were forced to make its acquaintance again. In cities like Memphis, whole neighborhoods that had been a thriving means of rising economic expectation just two years before were suddenly a Wild West of hyper-slums, foreclosed homes, and drug houses. How do you argue to the people of those cities that they were ever really citizens of something? And if they in their millions are not citizens, who is? The city is not merely the location for this drama. This drama is the city.

Apologists are fond—as they always are—of pointing out how much things have improved since the nineteenth century. How government has made laissez-faire market anarchy behave responsibly through labor law, aggressive taxation of corporate profits, the provision of public schools, and social welfare. But then one reads of the new industrial cities of China, like Shenzhen (one of China's Special Economic Zones modeled after Hong Kong). There, Foxconn industry employs 400,000 people assembling products for Apple and other computer companies. Assembly line employees work seventy-five hours a week for the equivalent of a dollar an hour and sleep in crowded dormitories with strangers. An increasing number of Chinese workers have come to see their free time as an opportunity to climb to the top of their dormitories and jump off. (If you own an iPhone, your relationship with those suicides may be more intimate than you know.) Many of those dormitories now come with enormous nets as standard safety equipment. But Shenzhen is not monstrous—it is merely typical of the cities of the last two centuries, in all of which suicide has been an all-too-familiar companion. We have exported not only our industries but our *cities* to the "developing" world. Shenzhen is an American city.

The American city has no problems that are its own because, in the last analysis, our cities aren't cities at all. They are structures for the maintenance of social inequality. This fact makes painfully comic the long history of reformers lamenting the wickedness of the city: gambling, drunkenness, profanity, prostitution, and Sabbath breaking. That these reformers were often local business leaders makes the joke delicious. And the enduring game of blaming the victims persists to this day, with the problems of inner-city drug- and gang-related crime, which can only be fixed by experts. (Paul Romer's expert opinion is that in the charter city of the future, people who are not disciplined and productive simply won't be allowed in. The poor and the criminal and the suicidal will have to look elsewhere for a bed.)

What is remarkable is that, blatant though this reality is, so few people seem capable of remembering it from moment to moment and soon retreat to the familiar homilies about fallen morality, personal responsibility, stiffer prison sentences, and *the inherent wickedness of the city.* This is what makes the HBO series *The Wire* so spectacularly unique; it never for an episode forgets that the problem of poverty, violence, and drugs in Baltimore was an expression of inhuman profit seeking and political corruption on the other side of town. The murderous immorality of the drug gangs themselves was merely more of the same. Drug boss "Stringer" Bell's lectures to his pushers on product quality, supply and demand, and Robert's Rules of Order are among the great televisual moments in the comédie humaine. In the end, there is no Baltimore; there is only "bizness."

And yet we love the city, and we are drawn there, in spite of all the ways in which it breaks our hearts. Why, exactly? If the city as we have known it is fundamentally an expression of capitalism's technological, economic, and social imperatives (and it is), the things that we are fond of in the city are basically ironies in the techno-capitalist order. The things that we love about the city are things that the city would love to destroy. Those things are:

Democracy: the self-awareness of people that they share ideas and interests, and that it is possible to give political force to those shared interests. (However disappointed we might now be, the 2008 election of Barack Obama was substantially the work of urban democracy, and Occupy Wall Street was its labor of love.)

Education: not just educational institutions, but a self-informing and self-reinforcing richness that happens when people are brought together in numbers. In the city, people teach

each other: read this book, listen to this music, go to this event. Perhaps the most useful thing they teach one another is skepticism ("Don't believe the hype").

And *art*: nowhere is the city's educational energy more intense than among those who have come to the city to be near art and artists. This bohemian culture rebels against the rigid policing of daily life. It models a form of freedom that is a natural antagonist to the culture of work and regimentation. Ironically, no one has found this culture more attractive and energizing than the bourgeois class itself, which buys its work, attends its ritual displays, and wraps itself in its sense of life. The life of art informs the educated pleasures of the city: bookstores, cafés, galleries, and restaurants. For the aficionado of the city, it is these pleasures that make the success of Barnes & Noble, Starbucks, and franchise eateries like the Olive Garden so painful.

As Lewis Mumford put it, "It is through the performance of creative acts, in art, in thought, in personal relationships, that the city can be identified as something more than a purely functional organization of factories and warehouses, barracks, courts, prisons, and control centers." Art is the city's "still unfulfilled promise."

Democracy, education, art: it's as if an ancient Greek dream still slept within the city. A dream in which the countryside and the city were not opposed and not different. A dream in which the city and nature are one. It is a dream of *nature's city* because it participates, as Schiller encouraged, in *nature's freedom*.

The things that we know as cities are not worthy of our

love. We should abandon the fantasy, the delusion of a dying culture, that through technical planning we can somehow fix the city. This is to condemn the city, as Fritz Lang did in the movie *Metropolis*, as a vast mechanism. What brings down the machine city is the machine soul (Maria's robot double) that is its last expression. Through robot-Maria the machine conspires against itself and brings about its own ruin.

The Romantics were not opposed to science and machines, but they were opposed to the machine soul—the human that believes it is a machine. We should try instead to make human places, in human proportions, for human purposes. We should make places that anticipate occupation by human *bodies* and not places that are vast, vain prosthetics for every human function. Everyone knows this, even city planners, although their vision of the humanized city tends not to extend beyond a pedestrian mall bracketed by parking garages in which cars are instructed "This Far But No Further" and walkers are granted the peculiar blessing of a postage stamp of green space.

The Occupy movement had one very notable success: bringing together the three activities of the true polis, nature's city, in one powerful political action. The desire and the capacity to revive the city will be the work of powers whose origins are in the city itself: democracy, education, and art. This is a gift, of course, that the industrial city never intended. Nevertheless, our hope must be that in the end, as Hegel put it, the city "meant something other than it meant to mean."

PARDON MY REVERIE

The preceding account of nature's city ignores the following irony: as we know, many of the contemporary city's "hipsters"—those who live through its educative pleasures—are themselves engineers, programmers, designers, etc. They work for Google or for one of the thousands of technology start-ups in cities across the country. As rural areas of the country depopulate, the people are not all going to San Francisco and Seattle. Even Des Moines, Iowa, has a growing population of the urban young looking for employment and lifestyle on "Silicon Sixth" Avenue. Young college graduates are moving not just to the usual places but also to cities like Denver, San Diego, Nashville, Salt Lake City, and Portland, Oregon. This is what Richard Florida has been predicting for many years: the triumph of the "creative economy."

This would also seem to support Tyler Cowen's predictions about the machine economy of the future. Some of these young workers come to the city to work in tech, and some of them come to work in areas that provide services to the tech workers, especially in culture and recreation (ethnic restaurants,

craft breweries, music scenes, ski instruction, all of the many
resourceful enterprises of the Entourage Economy). But after
a certain point, it is unclear which is the real driving force:
the work or the culture. In places like Des Moines it would
seem that for the moment the two are happily leapfrogging
each other; the tech companies provide economic activity that
is followed by cultural enhancements, which then makes the
city more attractive to yet more tech companies, which again
enlarges the demand for restaurants, bike shops, and art centers. Of course, most of these start-ups are running on highly
speculative investment capital and do not actually have established products, let alone profits—and so Silicon Sixth is only a
bad Wall Street week away from being Sell-off Sixth should the
creative economy turn out to be a creative bubble.

  And yet, a revealing detail: high-end bicycle mechanics. In
this economy, they can pretty much live anywhere they want
fixing beautifully engineered state-of-the-art bicycles by companies like Specialized, Trek, and Cannondale (to name only
American manufactures). Most of these mechanics are young
people who are passionate about cycling, and though they
make only $23,000 per year on average, they dress as they like,
play Animal Collective at an acceptable volume in the shop,
and really don't seem to resent the customers who can actually
buy the bikes they fix but can't afford to buy themselves, like
the Specialized S-Works Venge. But it's all good, because the
customers who can afford the Venge also like Animal Collective, and share the mechanic's taste for imperial IPA, which

they happily doff in comradely quantities after Tuesday night training rides.*

So perhaps this is one of the ways in which engineers and bohemians, capitalists and artists, have a happy meeting of minds. Perhaps it is only a matter of time until the natural evolution of this benign conspiracy of economic forces makes the engineered city's problems disappear beneath a swathe of green belts, urban trails, and local breweries. This is exactly how Richard Florida sees it: in an ideal creative economy, both freestyler and service provider will see that they are not enemies, not master and servant; they depend upon each other and are united together against the real villain—the corporation, the owners of the means of production. As Florida says in an interview with *Jacobin*'s Erin Schell:

> I'd say the central contradiction of capitalism . . . is the attempt to impose top-down order, corporate direction, corporate control over the full flourishing of human creativity—this conflict between organization and creativity.
>
> If Marx saw the working class as the universal class, I think the creative class—the notion that every human being is creative—is an even broader class.

Very much in this vein, some neo-Marxist sociologists theorize that the proletariat is no longer the unique historical antagonist to capitalism. In an uncannily prescient book written in 1982, *The Future of Intellectuals and the Rise of the New Class*,

---

* Here in Bloomington-Normal, Illinois, the systems analysts from State Farm Insurance ride with the gear-heads in what we call the Tuesday Night Worlds.

Alvin W. Gouldner describes a new "universal class"—the New Class—composed of technocrats and humanist intellectuals. They share the same educational experiences, the same elite cultural influences, and the same heightened social consciousness (environmentalism, human rights, etc.). It's pretty to think so, but nothing remotely resembling this has appeared in the years since Gouldner's book. Rather, we have seen something more like Theodore Roszak's pessimistic account written in 1967:

> Both humanist and technician can take pride in their joint product: let us say an Aerospace computer programmer. Off the job he is a man of easy culture. He listens appreciatively to his local "good music" station; his library is filled with paperback editions of Plato, Tolstoy, Shakespeare; his walls are graced with Modigliani and Braque prints. He remembers his Humanities 1A and his English Lit. 44B, and they decorate his life. On the job, he complacently and ingeniously perfects the balance of terror.

Perhaps Sixth Avenue in Des Moines and even downtown Buffalo will become what Harvard economist Edward Glaeser calls "the triumph of the city." Yet none of this would appear to help that half of the working population that has failed to become either an engineer or an artista (as in barista). They will live in rural areas that will feel increasingly emptied of everyone except an aging population of the irrelevant and a growing population of Latinos and other immigrant labor willing to face the horror of a Tyson meatpacking plant in, for example, Tipton, Iowa, where—not inconveniently—half the town is ineligible to vote. To be sure, Des Moines still has its own meat-packing factories (there are a total of 130 in Iowa), but that only serves to show how the United States has become essentially two economies: a first-world economy driven by technicians and their various entourages, and a third-world economy driven by immigrants and, increasingly, the forlorn folks who were formerly our pride, the salt of the earth, the hearty denizens of the American heartland. Americans in name, they have been priced out of the American economy.

But from the perspective of techno-economists like Cowen and Romer, *that's okay*. It's okay because their thought seeks the following: an economy dominated by high-end consumption; cities that are technological marvels full of highly sophisticated human pleasures; and hyperbolic power, wealth, and cult-like prestige for the uber-creatives like Steve Jobs and Bill Gates. *That* is the world they want, and they are well on their way to having it.*

---

* High-end consumption: New York City's sophisticates spent over $25 billion in 2014, more than the whole of Japan, the second-largest consumer of luxury goods. As for yachts, the last time we saw them they were floating listlessly in harbors up and down the New England coast waiting for bankruptcy seizure. Well, they're à la mode these days along with customized "super cars." Or how about a $100,000 artisanal bed from Manhattan's Hastens, the Swedish mattress company? As for personal luxuries, for the first time since 2007 the sales of luxury footwear exceeded the entirety of the remaining leather goods market. Come back, Imelda Marcos, all is forgiven. And what are the techies buying? At the top of *Wired*'s 2014 Christmas wish list was the Lazy Suzi 66 "hypnotic spinning centerpiece" for the dinner table ($525). Or your loved ones might be happy to receive the Breville Oracle Espresso Machine ($2,000), Fujifilm's X-T1 ($1,199 lens not included), or the MartinLogan Crescendo Wireless Speaker (a "crescent of sonic perfection" at $900). This is the payoff for those long days editing software manuals in the corporate coop.

#Art-Bot

What does shock one horribly is this mixture in the works of Dumas and other writers of an exaggerated realism abhorrent to the arts, and of sentiment, characters and situations of the most false and extravagant kind . . . If these men were sculptors, they would paint their statues and have them fitted with springs to enable them to walk, and believe that by so doing they are getting nearer to the truth.

—Eugene Delacroix,
The Journal of Eugene Delacroix

Americans love junk. It's not the junk that bothers me, it's the love.

—George Santayana*

COMPOSING YOUR NOSEGAY IS YOUR OWN AFFAIR

As the quote above from Eugene Delacroix suggests, robotic art has been around a long time. It reached its height during the mid-nineteenth century in the art movement called Naturalism. In literature, Naturalism employed what it took to be aspects of the scientific method—objectivity, causal determinism—in

---

* This is probably an apocryphal citation.

order to depict characters who were seen as helpless products of heredity and environment, motivated by instinctual drives. In short, a deterministic world full of "biochemical puppets" (Sam Harris). For such a famous movement, Naturalism had few great practitioners with the exception of Émile Zola, "a large enough figure to make us lose time in walking round him for the most convenient view," as Henry James wrote. When James found a view, it was not flattering: Zola, and Naturalism with him, were not capable of much more than the vigorous application of a method: "None of M. Zola's heroes stands so squarely on their feet as M. Zola's heroic system."

Naturalism's outsized claims for its "science" did not long survive the perspicacity of critics like James, less still the guffaws of Surrealism and Dada, but its longing for objectivity, for the *adequacy* of the word to the world, remain with us to this day in that literary form we know as realism. For the vast majority of American writers, the idea that literature is only about as-ifs and playful invention—and not about Truth—is unpalatable, amoral, relativistic, and even un-American. To this day, the realist novelist is expected to discover something true about "who we are," as if that were a stable and knowable quantity that is for some reason being kept secret. More important, realism is trusted to provide the *same thing*, the same attitude toward reality, over and over again, and, to make matters even better for the status quo, it will produce the same thing over and over through an epistemology that is compatible with the realist assumptions of science. When employed in this way,

literary realism provides an appropriate art form for a quantified soul living in a machine world.

Many bloody-minded words have been spilled in the last
fifty years over the ongoing Battle of the Books that we know
as realism vs. postmodernism. My sympathies have always been
with the innovators, but that does not mean that I dismiss realism as a literary technique. As a kind of fiction-making, realism has wonderful capacities on which even the most meta- of
meta-fictional novelists are happily dependent when it suits
them. But in a culture dominated by empirical and mechanistic
thought, there is always the danger that we will forget that realism is itself an as-if—"what if words could accurately imitate/
reflect personal and social reality"—and begin treating it as a
form of truth-making. The problem comes when someone like
Tom Wolfe in his 1989 *Harper's Magazine* essay "Stalking the
Billion Footed Beast," or Jonathan Franzen in "Perchance to
Dream: In the Age of Images, Reasons to Write Novels" (1996,
also *Harper's Magazine*), argues that social realism is *truer* (because it is more objectively based) and therefore morally superior to other forms of fiction-making.

I have never understood the logic behind this claim, but I
assume that it goes something like this: 1) Language is capable
of mirroring/representing objective reality. (This is where this
logic must start, the problem being that it is an enormously
naïve and philosophically unsupportable proposition. But onward!) 2) Literary realism uses language to represent social reality. 3) Postmodern or otherwise experimental fiction does not

use language in this way. It conceives that language refers only to itself. 4) Therefore, postmodernism is not interested in reality, especially the values that animate human reality. 5) Therefore, it is immoral, or, at best, not interested in what is moral.

If writers don't conform to this logic, their work will be seen as deviant, immoral, and, as agents and editors like to say, non-commercial. As Dubravka Ugrešić writes in *Thank You for Not Reading*:

> The literary market demands that people adapt to the norms of production. As a rule, it does not tolerate disobedient artists, it does not tolerate experimenters, artistic subversives, performers of strange strategies in a literary text. It rewards the artistically obedient, the adaptable, the diligent, those who respect literary norms . . . In the literary industry, writers are obedient workers, just a link in the chain of production.

I want to emphasize that this is not about easy conflicts—about what is the better kind of fiction and who are the better writers. It may be that official literary culture has been unfair to the sizable talent of the so-called postmodern fiction writers, but that is not the point. The point, as I have argued here throughout, is that the fictiveness of our world itself isn't going away. The world remains "made of stories." What goes away, under the unrelenting hostility of mainstream literary culture, is the *self-awareness* that the world is made of stories. So-called "metafiction" is one of the most important ways in which storytellers maintain a critical distance on the act of storytelling, so that we are not led to believe that our fabrications are Truth.

Without this self-awareness, we are more likely to accept the prevarications of ideologues. We are more likely to believe them when they say that their stories are not stories but reality. Tyler Cowen does not encourage us to think that his account of the economy of the future is a fiction. He wants us to think that it is real and therefore inevitable. It is a great convenience to ideologues like Cowen that philosophy like Vaihinger's is not present in any important way in the culture: it makes his job easier.

•

> The conventional way of telling stories is itself a kind of religion, you know, a dogmatic belief in a certain type of human perception as the only valid one. Like religious people, conventional writers follow hand-me-down catechisms and look upon the human story through a particular narrow lens . . . The true realists are the lens-breakers.
> —SALLY ELLIOTT, IN ROBERT COOVER'S
> *The Brunist Day of Wrath*

•

The worst thing about the Wolfe/Franzen position is that it is not a defense of realism, but a betrayal. When Henry James concluded that the ultimate sin for a novelist is to admit that the story is a story (and therefore unreal), he did not mean that novelists are under any illusions about it. Novelists know the story is a story. (James himself was fond of making his novels by elaborating fragmentary anecdotes heard at the dinner table; so he was well aware of the tenuous relation of fiction to reality.) When putative realist Joseph Conrad used the old salt Marlow to narrate *The Heart of Darkness*, he knowingly inserted a level of irony and unreliability into his tale. The reader should ask: Can Marlow be trusted? Is he another crazy swabby? Does he represent Conrad's perspective? These questions are made even more necessary by the fact that Conrad loved to use doppelgängers, or doubles, in his work in order to show how one character—in this case, Marlow—sees aspects of himself in a morally compromised character like the murderous rogue colonialist Mr. Kurtz. And Marlow, in turn, is Conrad's double. Through Marlow, Conrad examines his own contradictory hatred of British imperialism even while being tempted and tainted by its odious assumptions about European superiority.

Conrad had more interesting things to do than worry about whether or not his readers would view Marlow as a verisimilar sailor, so to speak. (He is in truth a hyperbolic sailor.) More than anything else, *The Heart of Darkness* is about complicity: judging the bad while fearing you are one of them.* This manipulation of a well-established trope—the doppelgänger—makes *The Heart of Darkness* self-aware and self-reflexive in a way that, we're told by the advocates of realism, novels shouldn't be. It is not solely concerned with the morality of colonialism; it is also concerned with how a Western novelist

---

* *The Heart of Darkness* was published in the first year of the First Boer War (1899). Mr. Kurtz's "unsound methods" were soon to be taken up in the Second Boer War (a guerrilla war) by Lord Kitchener, the commanding officer of British forces. Kitchener's policy of placing the women and children of Boer guerrillas in concentration camps and feeding them only half rations was essentially an order to, as Kurtz put it, "exterminate all the brutes." ("Obey me and be happy, or die," Conrad wrote in *An Outcast of the Islands* [1896]. And die they did.)

can write about colonialism and not be implicated in what he depicts.

The ironic distance between Conrad and the artifice of his stories approaches postmodern parody in works like *Romance*, in which Conrad (with Ford Maddox Ford) plows through all the hoary clichés of the adventure story (including a youth's abduction by pirates) and yet creates something that is deeply compelling. It is a self-conscious novel about a kind of novel, *and* it is a virtuoso example of the type. Conrad understood what Aristotle understood: mimesis—the representation of reality in art—is not about the imitation of the outside world; it is about the imitation of "acceptable" literary forms, especially those that support the dominant beliefs of a given culture. But *Romance* both provides what is acceptable (a romantic adventure story) and laughs at it, as if to say this is malarkey, of course, but it's magnificent malarkey. *Romance* is deviant. It employs a trick that was typical of the so-called American postmodernists, and yet Conrad is regularly assumed to be a realist (or "romantic realist"), one of those great canonical writers who can be used to pummel the experimenters.

The truth is that all novelists are to some degree reporters on experience and to another degree they are manipulators of artifice. A novelist who doesn't understand this is a very stupid novelist indeed. In that sense, Tolstoy and Conrad, Kafka and Joyce all stand on the same terrain, although allowances must be made for the respective bevel of said terrain. Even Henry James was loath to say there was any way fiction *ought* to be done. In "The Art of Fiction," he writes, "Humanity is immense and reality has a myriad forms; the most one can affirm is that some of the flowers of fiction have the odor of it, and others have not; as for telling you in advance how your nosegay should be composed, that is another affair."

REALITY ANXIETY DISORDER

My own preferred point of philosophical reference for resolving the supposed incompatibility of reality and artifice is French philosopher Paul Ricoeur's magnificent *Time and Narrative, Volume I*. It is an imposing work, but its ideas are both lucid and compelling. For Ricoeur, the problem of realism has little to do with either the real or the artificial. The problem has to do with what is familiar and what is unfamiliar; acceptable and unacceptable; consonant and dissonant.

The logic of his position goes like this:

He writes, "Time becomes *human* time to the extent that it is organized after the manner of a narrative." An obvious example: we impose the idea that things happen with a beginning, middle, and end on events that would otherwise be formless. Or we read about the deeds of heroes (protagonists), and that teaches us to look for heroes and villains in real events. American foreign policy is, unfortunately, all about labeling people as "friends" or "evildoers," Abu Bakr al-Baghdadie of ISIS being the most recent example.

But these narratives are not static; in fact, they are inherently unstable, naturally, since they are only stories. Most important, they oscillate between what Ricoeur terms concordance and discordance. In concordance, communities repeat their central myths, the stories that make them a "cult" and give them an identity, in order to provide a sense of social continuity. And so Americans tell themselves their "founding" stories over and over again, even though some of them are quite deranged and self-destructive: how the Founding Fathers were the homogenous embodiment of wisdom (when in fact they hated one another, mostly along Federalist and Republican lines); how these wise fathers created a Christian nation "under God" (when in fact many of them—Jefferson, Paine, Franklin—were Deist skeptics); how the Second Amendment means that we all have the right to carry assault rifles; and how everyone should strive for the American Dream understood as "success," that "American bitch goddess" (William James), and so on. Deranged though they may be, these stories are comforting for many Americans, and to challenge them is to invite vigorous debate if not a fistfight.

At a more sophisticated level, readers take a similar comfort from the conventions of realism. Realist fiction provides a way of feeling that we know who we are, we know this world, we know this particular way of constructing time, etc. It is reassuring. The consonance of the realist world with what we take to be the world we actually live in provides a way of refiguring, generation after generation, what is known and therefore virtuous. As Ian Watt long ago discovered in his book *The Rise of the*

Novel, the realist novel's uncomplicated appropriation of both empiricism and middle-class verities has made it the dominant storytelling mode for bourgeois culture.

For American culture, the conventions of the realist novel are an enormous feedback loop. It is as if the reader were saying, "You have taught me to expect these conventions, and I do. In fact, I demand them. If you don't give them to me, I will complain loudly." This is, perhaps, a little noticed form of obsessive-compulsive disorder. We expect the world to be in the way we have been told that it is, but we are anxious that it might not be in that way, and so we seek reassurance through repetition. "Weird" novels (as my students always insisted on calling innovative writing) threaten our sense of who we are. Realism is thus no longer merely a literary technique, one among many; it is a way to make everything okay for those of us afflicted with Reality Anxiety Disorder (RAD).

THE NOVEL OF THE FUTURE WILL HAVE A BILLION VISITORS

Now, you might think that in our technologically advanced, hipper-than-thou age of guru blogsters and *Wired* orthodoxy, we would be accustomed to having our reality shaken and we'd be in RAD remission. This is the era, after all, of crowdsourcing and Kickstarting and not of the Writers Guild. Oddly, while the technology may be disruptive, the psychological reality behind the technology appears to be all too familiar. (I noted something similar to this earlier when I observed that the cyber economy seems to have derived its work ethic from the usual Protestant sources.)

For example, at the website "Authonomy" administered by HarperCollins, readers can rate manuscripts that are submitted to the site (at present, there are 100,000 users and 15,000 submissions). Awesome, right? But the kicker is that authors are using this input in order to fine-tune their work to their readers' expectations. For example, Sandy Hall, a young adult writer, published her first novel, *A Little Something Different*, only after revising it based upon suggestions submitted by online readers. Hall commented: "Having had it tested online, you can really tailor it to what people want to read." Just ask fan-fiction author Anna Todd, author of the 2,500-page novel *After*, who said of her composition habits, "The only way I know how to write is socially and getting immediate feedback on my phone."* As of October 2014, *After* had been viewed more than a billion times on the free fiction site Wattpad, and Todd had a six-figure multibook deal with literary gatekeeper Simon & Schuster, as well as a film option with Paramount.†

---

* It may help to recall the lyrics to the Beatles' "Paperback Writer":

> *I can make it longer if you like the style*
> *I can change it round and I want to be a paperback writer.*

† Much the same thing is, apparently, made possible by the algorithms on the music streaming service Spotify. According to a 2015 *Wired* article, one Matt Farley, a counselor to troubled teens by day, writes 200 songs per month and makes them available through Spotify. He has written more than 16,000 songs in the last seven years. (He has a 92-song album about staplers.) Last year, he made $27,000 while real musicians (not named Kanye or Beyoncé) struggled to make more than they could get by selling a T-shirt at a concert.

It goes without saying that what the readers of this fiction want to read is something like what they've already read—i.e., realism and genre fiction. Using these protocols, *A Little Something Different* is by definition not different at all. Or it had better not be if she wants to publish another book!

Or consider the work of Chicago-based "Collabowriters" who are (which is?) writing the first Internet novel by painstakingly crowdsourcing the work one anguished sentence at a time. Here is the first product of their collective genius:

> The barbed sweet stenches of sewage wafting up between the ice cracks on the canal were arrogantly broadcasting an early spring. From somewhere across the canal, a soft sound was barely audible over the moan of shifting ice and garbage: "Help." Zachary stopped, at first unsure of what he had heard.

For all its hypertextual bravado, this is familiar stuff, as familiar as teenaged boys hunched around computers eating Volcano Nachos at Taco Bell.

Of course, to say that what motivates this new breed of cloud-based writer is a commitment to a realist epistemology gives them far too much credit. What they are responding to is a market. And in the end the market drives their creations in much the same way that Stalin drove socialist realism. Again, Dubravka Ugrešić:

> [Under Stalin] writers who were unable to adapt to the demands of the ideological market ended tragically: in camps.

Nowadays, writers who cannot adapt to commercial demands end up in their own personal ghetto of anonymity
and poverty.

Here, writers may say anything they want as long as it doesn't
matter. A book burning holds no terror for this country. There's
not much left to burn.

INHERITED STUPIDITY

Unfortunately, being reassured and comforted by the repetition of what is familiar also has the effect, as Nietzsche put it,
of "gradually increasing inherited stupidity." Stupidity haunts
consonance and creates, in Nietzsche's words, "fettered souls."
The measure of a community's truths is their utility; any unfet-
tered souls who say deviant things and threaten the stability of
these useful truths are wrong not because they can be shown
to be wrong but because they are thought to be harmful to the
community. They are thought to be lacking in virtue at best
and evildoers at the margin. Sunni extremists are not the only
people worried about infidels, about those who are unfaith-
ful to a culture's assumptions/virtues. The postmodern fiction
writer that Tom Wolfe loves to hate is an infidel.

NARRATIVE AS DIALECTIC

In a healthy culture, which ours obviously is not, our social
narratives will change, sometimes dramatically. The problem is

to explain how repetition and change can be part of the same process. How does concord relate to discord, consonance to dissonance? Is it simply that they are antagonists? Or are they dependent on one another in some way?

If you think about it, discord is fundamental even to the most concordant/acceptable realist drama. It is the moment in which the familiar is suddenly challenged by a threat or a reversal of what is familiar. In conventional plotting, this is the idea that a "normal day" is interrupted by "complication" (a threat to normalcy, a threat to homeostasis), followed by "rising action" (which gradually builds tension), and "crisis." Sherlock Holmes is in his study, he's playing the violin, Watson is smoking and reading the paper in an armchair—then, shockingly, there is a knock at the door. A man with a knife in his back stumbles in carrying a package. A seductive woman enters, her face veiled, smoking a cigarette. Or here comes an odd foreign fella of uncertain sexual disposition with a little gun. (Oh, sorry, that's *The Maltese Falcon*. But you get the idea.) Our sense of the normal is threatened. The "pleasure of the text" is in "suspending" this unease for as long as possible before returning us, reassured, to the same study where Holmes can take up his partita just where he'd left off, or Sam Spade can put his feet up and roll a cigarette, Effie Perine perched on the desk to light it. This conventional narrative begins with discord, but in the end it is only another realist reassurance machine, antidote to Reality Anxiety Disorder, never mind that nothing could be more artificial and unreal than this supposed gritty realism.

It's like the story that Freud tells of a little boy, his grandson, who becomes anxious when his mother leaves the house. So he invents a game called *fort/da* (gone and there) to reassure himself of his mother's eventual return and thereby to master his anxiety. He throws a stringed toy away from him (*fort*) and then reels it back (*da*). Literary realism plays this game by unsettling the reader's sense of normalcy and then returning it to cultural homeostasis.

More disruptive than this game are those narratives that threaten the realist reassurance machine through the violence of the new: experimental novels, nonrepresentational art, and music without a clear key signature. They go *fort*, but they don't necessarily come *da*. And yet the anarchic and defamiliarizing work of art has been the norm in art movements since the Romantics. Is the sonata form a prison? Write Beethoven's Fifth, and when the Fifth becomes a prison, write Schoenberg's *Pierrot Lunaire*. Is courtly portraiture an art for slaves? Paint Goya's "Black Paintings," and when even that starts to feel tame, paint Egon Schiele's splay-legged whores. Feel repressed by the sonnet? Write Wordsworth's *Prelude*, a veritable declaration of war on the world of the familiar, and when the *Prelude* no longer suffices, write Ezra Pound's *Cantos*. Has psychedelia been domesticated? Blow it up with the Ramones, Swans, and punk. Art movements tend not to want to have anything to do with bourgeois reassurance. Reality Disorder (with or without the anxiety) is their mother's milk.

But this still doesn't show how the two kinds of narrative

ought ideally to work together. Ricoeur proposes that we add a third term and create a dynamic (or dialectical) relationship among the three. He calls this arrangement threefold mimesis (M1, M2, and M3). That sounds thornier than it is. M1 is the moment of the prefigured; the world we happened to be born into that provides individuals with a culture—whether American or Talibani—or a "pre-understanding" of what will count as real/normal. (This is Nietzsche's "inheritance.") M2 is the moment of configuration, the writer's moment. Here, the writer can choose to confirm M1 or challenge it to some degree, whether modest or revolutionary. This provides narrative with dynamism, and thus the possibility for change. Finally, M3 is the reader's moment, the moment of refiguration. The reader/listener/viewer can find solace in the conventional configuration of the text, or react in outrage if the text refuses to confirm (creating the scandal of *Ubu Roi*, *The Rites of Spring*, or the lewd expressionist paintings of *der Blaue Reiter*), or she can embrace the scandal of the new as so many thousands embraced the self-destructive scandal of French Symbolism in the 1880s or punk in the 1980s. Speaking for such scandals, George W. S. Trow wrote:

> As the boy slices his skin to watch a scar form, he thinks how loathsome and intolerable life was before he thought to do it, and how comforting it is to belong to the new aristocracy of people who have had the imagination to have an intention to wound themselves.

Usually, the embrace of deviance comes not because of some innate perversity but because of a preexisting dissatisfaction with the world as it stands acquired through alienating experiences of one sort or another.* Dissident artists offer consolation to the already alienated through the experience of the work of art understood as utopian longing for a future (and better) world. They offer the possibility of freedom and happiness in a reconfigured world. But first the world as it stands must be blown up (metaphorically). For example, the radical otherness of psychedelia or the art rock of Sonic Youth can lead us to reject the world of parents and authority, and it can lead us to embrace an urban "scene" (the East Village), an "underground," or a subculture (the Grateful Dead's Dead Nation, morphing into Burning Man, is probably the most famous example), all instances of the politics of non-participation—not just off-the-energy grid or the media grid or the money grid, but off-the-grid grid. More often than not, this embrace of deviant art (as Hitler accurately called it) is a minority affair, but it can also grow to be a serious challenge, especially if it coincides with a political crisis (World War I, Vietnam) or if it finds a way to ally itself with a student or labor movement (like the Autonomia movement in Italy in the 1970s). Remember, when imagination "took power" in France in May '68 in alliance with artists, intellectuals, students, and workers, Charles DeGaulle felt so threatened that he fled—he *fled the country* (for Germany, of

---

* As Stephen Daedalus commented in Joyce's *Ulysses*: "I'd rather have my country die for me." A very punk sentiment.

all places) as if the students were the second coming of the Nazi wehrmacht.

Ricoeur concluded that the best way to understand the social function of narrative was as "rule-governed deformation." Narrative doesn't only repeat what is acceptable; it is also "productive." Narrative is the dynamic relationship between "sedimentation" and innovation. Narrative is neither realism nor experimentation: it is both.

It is for this reason that we live not only in loyalty to an inherited sense of order; we also live in fascination with the unformed and emergent. We want stability, but we also want what John Barth called the "best next thing." Order is our home, but it is a dead home, a prison, without the violence of innovation.

The big philosophical question for Ricoeur is where this dynamic is going. Is it a meaningless circling? Or is it going somewhere? Does it have a direction, a destination, a utopian Absolute? Ricoeur suggests that narrative is not a circle but a spring-shaped vortex that leads somewhere better and freer, but he offers no way to know that that is true. Wherever it might be heading, what Ricoeur describes is the way in which cultures evolve.

•

For the past million years, human culture has been the most important selective influence in making men what they are.
                                                —JACOB BRONOWSKI

•

ARID AND ACIDIC

At a May 2014 art auction run by Christie's, David Ganek, a hedge fund manager, put up a Twombly and a Warhol; Peter Brant sold canvases by Basquiat and Haring; Steve Wynn, the casino tycoon, a de Kooning; and Ronald O. Perelman, a Rothko. These days, such offerings from Christies are like the announcement of a bond sale from the Treasury Department.

Even Christie's expert employees, standing chin-deep in money and bad faith, are complaining. Brett Gorvy commented, "The mind-set and perspective of these people have changed. It used to be that collectors rarely plotted the value of their art the same way they do their homes or stock portfolios, but more and more people are looking at their collections in the same terms as other assets."

The romance of the collector is gone and has been replaced (much longer ago than Mr. Gorvy allows) by an interest in a work's "trajectory" as an investment instrument. Global sales of art and antiquities topped $68 billion in 2013. Most museums have been priced out of this market and replaced by a small world of bidders willing to pay $25–$50 million for one work.

As Christine Smallwood observed in a *Harper's Magazine* review of Don Thompson's *The Supermodel and the Brillo Box*:

> The art world is more than a confidence game—it's an
> unregulated money market in which galleries and auction
> houses provide loans to consignors and collectors. The "free"
> market operates here much as it does elsewhere, by being
> propped up and framed. Auction prices are routinely bid

up by interested collectors like Mugrabis and dealers like
Larry Gagosian, who don't want the value of their holdings
to decline. So much is concentrated in so few hands that the
threat of a dump must be, and is, continually warded off.

As Smallwood suggests, there is something uncertain and risky
about using art as an investment tool. True, but the art market
is uncertain in a different and much larger way; it is an unusu-
ally vivid example of the fragility of the entire world of capitalist values.

The artworks themselves are, of course, saturated with
meaning even if that meaning is silly, as is the case with many
of the priciest contemporary pieces at auction (Jeff Koons,
Keith Haring). Francis Bacon's triptych *Three Studies of Lucian
Freud* (which sold for $142 million in 2013 to casino magnate
Elaine Wynn) is demanding on its viewers: something disturbing and unpleasant must be imagined in a dark space beyond
the painting's surface. Not that such a demand matters much.
Most of the works sold at auction will find their way to private
hands and security vaults where their only likely viewer will be
a representative from Lloyds of London.

Perhaps the successful bidder, Elaine Wynn, is old-school,
an "art lover," maybe she even admires Bacon's depths, but
Three Studies' value at auction, the reason she had to bid $42
million *over* the Christie's estimate, was that it was a famous
painter's painting of a famous painter who happened to be the
grandson of Sigmund Freud. Believe it or not, this story of the
"fame" of the painting's historical associations is the collateral,

the guarantee, for an investment of nearly $150 million. But the lines that formed outside the Portland Art Museum, to which Wynn loaned the paintings after her purchase, were mostly attracted by the fame of a painting that is worth so much money. As Philip Kennicott quipped of the *Triptych* in *The Washington Post*: "It is now famous for being expensive, rather like some people are famous for being famous."

The most intensely value-laden artifacts of human creativity—works of art—are now the purest examples of that old capitalist alchemy: turning human value into exchange value. At a certain point, and that point has been passed, the art market will be only a mathematical exchange. Art is worth money, but what's money worth? Money is the ultimate numbers game.* What the furor over the art market brings tantalizingly close to the surface is the fact that it is not just the value of art that is dependent on a shared fantasy, it is also money itself.

Warhol is not the name of an artist, it is the name of a currency. "Warhol" is a big number because its denomination (soup cans, Brillo box simulacrums, etc.) is presumed to be stable and growing. But it can inflate and deflate like any stock or bond or national currency. Jeff Koons is also a currency but less stable. The only thing that really changes hands are numbers that are for some reason associated with these opaque talismans called

---

* Placing this game where it probably belongs, in numerology; it is rumored that the lot number of the Bacon was changed because of a Chinese bidder. As Don Thompson (cited above) reports, "The painting was originally listed as lot 32 in the catalog, but they moved it up to lot 8A. Apparently they had a Chinese bidder who was very interested, but he'd only bid if it was item No. 8, because 8 is a lucky number."

"artworks." The billionaire buyers of these works have been reduced to South Sea natives who insist on the magical properties
of certain queer objects—a cornhusk doll with pearls for eyes
and a colorful ribbon about its head—but are unable to say why
they are so important or why their world would collapse without them. Investors in the art market need to fear not only the
economic boogies of bubbles and ponzi schemes but also that
dreaded moment when they look at one another in panic and
say, "What were we thinking? What is this stuff? What could
have possessed us to say that a glass balloon dog is worth tens
of millions? Sell! Sell!"

The art market is a ponzi scheme but with a difference. Like
a ponzi scheme, people are asked to invest in property that has
no real value, and trading continues until the scheme falls apart
and the last man holding the asset (that voodoo-lookin' Basquiat scrawl that he—oops—paid $13 million for) loses his
shirt. The difference is that everyone who participates in the
scheme knows that the assets have no real value, or nothing remotely like the absurd sums that are being spent on them. They
simply hope that they won't be the one to get burned. (Remember musical chairs?) The only plausible reason for investor
confidence is in the fact that the store of multimillion-dollar
artworks is concentrated among such a small number of investors that the uber-rich won't allow the market to fail. They'll
bid failing pieces up in order to protect the cache of "a Warhol."
They are like those corporations in the 1929 crash that sought
to support share price by buying their own eroding stock.

The maintenance of the capitalist order is dependent on a veritable 1,001 nights of stories whose purpose is only to inspire consent and thus legitimacy among the human beings subject to it, but what a Christie's art auction shows is that ideally capitalism would like to be free of all the storytelling baggage. They would prefer the purity of abstraction without all the idiot stories about famous paintings and their painters, something with the crisp, bracing mountain air they savor at Davos, Switzerland. At Davos, the super-rich are free to drop all pretense. There, art is cleansed of its human impurities, especially the aura of the artist.

Except that even in the privileged aery of Davos, they have to continue to tell one another that it's art and that art has an intrinsic value, that it has "beauty" or "importance." These are, obviously, empty tautologies. Nevertheless, they must continue to tell a story about being the connoisseurs, the ones who know, and that only they, the rightful owners of money, know how to perform the delicate operation that will express artistic beauty in dollars. The point is that art as a medium of exchange is, like money itself, precious *only because the masters say it is.*

This is such stupid and transparent hokum that in the dark night of the capitalist soul, they must feel confusion and fear. At some frightening level, the super-rich understand that so long as they must continue to tell such stories they will be vulnerable; they fear that someone will reveal that their magical power to confer value is only an illusion. There is no such thing as value; there is only the grift.

For the self-esteem of the rich, the devil of it all is that until they can stop telling these moron stories, they will not *feel* like masters of the universe, they will feel like people with dark secrets, losers and frauds waiting to be discovered. They can only be masters so long as they're hucksters; they can only be the boss if the suckers agree they are. But what a story they have to tell not only to themselves but also to the rest of humanity, the seven billion of us: "We are the lords! Art is precious because we say it is! We know which artworks are beautiful and which artworks are not! Therefore, the beautiful is worth hundreds of millions! Just one of these works is worth as much as all the buildings in your terrible little towns! So, look on us and fear!"

Intermission
The People of the Id

It would be pleasing to one's sense of enlightened amour pro-pre to know that the storytelling done by America's political progressives has no sins of its own to account for, no egregious lying machines smelling of propaganda, false consciousness, and the exploitation of the terminally foolish. We progressives would like to think that all of our as-if-ing is done through the innocence of the arts, through our utopian aspirations, and not inflicted on other people for our own benefit. That, unfortunately, is not the case.

Let me try to take account (with a sort of counter-contrarian flourish) of at least one of those leftish narrative strands. It is this: we left-leaners narrate poor, white, rural, conservative, Southern culture as if it were the world of the People of the Id. These People are, of course, not shy about labeling us, so-called

liberals, as sinners of one kind or another (humanists, relativ-
ists, heathens, homosexuals, baby killers, communists, in order
of increasing flammability), but we're not much conscious of
how we return the favor.

We return the favor by treating them as if they were primitive, violent, stupid, animalistic, and destructive. We treat
them as if they were children of Freud's secular Satan, the
dark Id. They are not, in our view, "evil" as such because their
faults seem so natural to them—so "native." But they do seem
immoral. That is, they seem to us to need an agency outside
of themselves to impose a little moral order, a little Law, on
them—by the scruff of the neck, if needed—just as we see on
the television show *COPS*.

We think of the People of the Id as a part of us, a part of our
own community that we must be vigilant against. They are a
part of us, but a part we must master. We think that they need
a little justice imposed on them. When the detective heroes of
HBO's 2014 *True Detective* impose the law on the pedophilic
monsters of rural Louisiana, they are clearly imposing the law
on people who are only a very small degree removed from themselves: poor, white, violent, drug- and alcohol-abusing people
who managed somehow to find a place on the "force." *True
Detective* is an allegory of morality understood as self-mastery.

But are the People of the Id aware that their unjust acts are
unjust? Sometimes, I suppose. From all appearances, there *are*
sociopaths out there happily acting out of "motiveless malignity." Our newspapers seem to be full of their wicked exploits,

staggering to contemplate. Take, for example, this one from October 2014:

> Four Fresno County teenagers were arrested Wednesday evening in connection with the golf-club slaughter of more than 900 chickens at a Foster Farms ranch south of Fresno, authorities said.

Hats off to the youth of Fresno on this one. I can't think of a motive for it, it doesn't fit into any notion of deviant culture that I can think of—even Voodoo takes it one chicken at a time—and it's clearly a malign thing that they did, although what Foster Farms had in mind for the chickens can't have been a lot better.*

But this sort of thing is not the behavior of the People of the Id, and neither is the sexual/religious derangement of Southern whites depicted on *True Detective*. Unlike the youth of Fresno, the People of the Id think that when they act they're *doing their duty*—they're doing what "anyone would do in my shoes." They think this even when very few people outside their community would do anything of the sort, never mind the shoes. In any case, the People of the Id feel quite innocent about their acts. "Nothin' special. Just standin' up for my rights," they say.

---

* Actually, according to investigations done by the Humane Society and others, getting whacked by a golf club might qualify as mercy in comparison with what industrial farming puts chickens through. Sure, the teens employed "unsound methods," but they just need the guidance of more experienced hands. Or perhaps Foster Farms should look on the boys as innovators and set them up with internships when they are paroled.

 Or perhaps it is all a misunderstanding: the boys were merely seeking to understand the poet Frank Stanford's immortal line "I have inhaled the fumes of the chicken feathers of death myself."

In other words, the People of the Id do what they're told they shouldn't do largely because they are under the impression that they are heroic, the defenders of all that is good, and certainly not people filled with motiveless malignity, a phrase that sounds to them like something that an overeducated elitist from San Francisco would say.

Should the People of the Id be called on their bad behavior, should their leaders be put in shackles, they are surprised, then outraged. Their friends and family members, their civic and religious leaders, turn and howl at the cameras. The very first thing they claim is that they, the valiant People of the Id, are the ones who have been treated unjustly, beginning with the fact that they have been treated like People of the Id, like a "common criminal," as they put it. They say, "We are not People of the Id, and we don't know where you got that idea. We are patriots. We are the real Americans. We are protecting the American Revolution from tyranny! You should be thanking us!"

I speak here of the Tea Party and the NRA. I speak of Hobby Lobby and Cracker Barrel. And at the extreme I speak of the White Aryan Resistance and the Creativity Movement.*

The problem is not that the People of the Id are bad; the problem is that there is another group of people called the People of the Law who call them bad. But the People of the Law are mistaken. Their mistake is in thinking that there is a difference

---

* Founded by Ben Klassen in 1974, the Creativity Movement advocated the worship of the white race before any deity. Klassen was an electrical engineer and the inventor of the wall-mounted electric can opener.

between the Id and the Law, a difference between the Id's putative destructiveness and the benign enforcement of the Law.
But they are in fact the same thing, *mutatis mutandis*. What the
People of the Id believe and too often act on, sometimes horribly, are the things that everyone around them—father, mother,
neighbor—has believed for decades if not centuries, and in this
they are no different from the People of the Law. The people
to whom love is owed have put them under a heavy *obligation* to believe certain stories, for the stories are nothing other
than their community's virtues. These virtues seem obvious to
them: "You can't tax me without my consent, you can't tell me
what kind of gun I can own, you can't tell me my daughter can
get an abortion, and you can't tell me two men can get married, not in Mississippi they can't." No wonder they think that
federal appeal courts are the instruments of the Antichrist.

When, as often happens, the People of the Id are told by
"outsiders" (those who bring the Law to them) that their truths
are lies and their virtues false, they become confused and in-
dignant. And should federal agents and troops come around to
enforce foreign virtues, it will seem as if they are being forced
to become members of a perverse community of evildoers, and
they don't wish to be perverse (they don't wish to be "preverts," as
Colonel "Bat" Guano [Keenan Wynn] put it in *Dr. Strangelove*).
They become angry because they can no longer experience the
pleasure of feeling at one with their world, and at one with that
world's unique sense of joy in living (even if this joy is predicated
on, for example, a tolerance for beating up gays on Saturday

night—that's just boys letting off steam and if the queers don't like it they should move to San Francisco—where they *belong*!).

It is for these reasons and more that we have in recent years experienced rancher-racist-patriot-hero-deadbeat Cliven Bundy and his armed and Stetson-hatted posse of seditionists. It is for these reasons that we have endured ugly-white-man-millionaire-NBA-franchise-owning-racist-with-diminished-mental-capacities Donald Sterling. And it is for these reasons that we have had no choice but to look into the eyes of oops-I-thought-y'all-was-Jews murderer Frazier Glenn Miller and wonder what dark mystery thrives therein.

We ask this man to pray for our forgiveness, but that makes no sense to him. "Forgive me my virtues!"—that is how he should pray!

When the People of the Id argue that they are merely living in a way that is consistent with the most ancient American traditions, traditions that have made them who they are, they are not wrong. As you may recall from high school history class, the Republican movement in this country was led by Thomas Jefferson and James Madison against the Federalists—in particular John Adams, with his fondness for courtly ritual, and the imperial Alexander Hamilton. The Republicans accused the Federalists of being aristocrats, elitists, and monarchists intent on establishing a strong central government, an exploitative system of excise taxes, a corrupt system of finance based on a permanent federal debt, and a standing military to enforce the government's autocratic whims. For Republicans, that sounded like being asked to pay for their own oppression.

Sound familiar?

But just as the Republican Party of the present has issues with Tea Party extremism, the Jeffersonians had their own problems with immoderation that came to a head in what was known as the Whiskey Rebellion. In brief, an excise tax to support the federal budget was placed on whiskey, which at that time was used by many farmers not only for local consumption but also as a kind of currency. Where were they going to get money to pay the taxes on the whiskey that they were using as money? (Perhaps they should have offered to give a few barrels to Hamilton and tell *him* to sell them if he wanted money.) Opposition to the tax in the West was so strong that a rebellion erupted in western Pennsylvania in which thousands of armed rebels organized, terrorized tax collectors, flew their own flag, and considered marching on the federal garrison in Pittsburgh. As our Tea Partiers of today would say, pennant in hand, "Don't tread on me!" But these activities only served to provoke exactly what they most feared: a federal military response brought down on their heads by Hamilton (gleefully) and Washington (resolutely).

And who were these rebels? The Federalists called them "busy and restless sons of anarchy," the anarchy consisting essentially in contempt for centralized lawmaking. These rebels were the first scofflaws, but they were also typical of rural

America at the time. As Gordon S. Wood describes our rustic forebearers in his book *Empire of Liberty: A History of the Early Republic, 1789–1815*:

> [N]early all Americans—men, women, children, and some-times even babies—drank whiskey all day long. Some work-ers began drinking before breakfast and then took dram breaks instead of coffee breaks. "Treating" with drink by mi-litia officers and politicians was considered essential to elec-tion. During court trials a bottle of liquor might be passed among the attorneys, spectators, clients, and the judge and jury . . . Whiskey accompanied every communal activity, including women's quilting bees.

And in the southern states, the men enjoyed chasing their whis-key with mortal combat:

> Men on the frontier often fought with "no holds barred," using their hands, feet, and teeth to disfigure or dismember each other until one or the other surrendered or was inca-pacitated. "Scratching, pulling hair, choking, gouging out each other's eyes, and biting off each other's noses" were all tried, recalled Daniel Drake, growing up in late eighteenth-century Kentucky. "But what is worse than all," observed the English traveller Isaac Weld, "these wretches in their combat endeavor to their utmost to tear out each other's testicles."

Hatred of the federal government, taxes, banks, and debt. A trust in the manly virtues of gun toting and whiskey. The embrace of extreme violence. Are the Tea Party, the NRA, and the avid fans of Xtreme Fighting mixed martial arts wrong to think that what they represent is not criminal but deeply, psy-

chically American? Are they not part of—even if a boundary-
pushing part—Jefferson's belief that the American experiment
had "the duty of proving what is the degree of freedom and
self-government in which a society may venture to leave its individual members"? Jefferson's assumption was that democracy
would cure itself; it did not need central regulation.

It's this simple: *Our modern People of the Id do not believe
that the degree to which they have taken freedom goes beyond that
place where a democratic society may venture.* It is for this reason
that they become so irate when a bureaucrat tells them that
they must wear a helmet when they ride a motorcycle, or that
they can't use a phone when they drive. Needless to say, the
list of things forbidden by federal and state law is not a short
one, as the prohibitions posted at our state and national parks
demonstrate, which is why it is rare to see one that has not been
improved with buckshot. Do the People of the Law want to
regulate head injuries in professional football? Do they want to
ban the NFL? To which the clever redneck ought to respond:
"Would you prefer going back to a time when the local sports
hero was an eye gouger and testicle tearer? What we are now is
a great refinement on what we were. We have established our
own limits without the intrusion of someone else's law. Yes,
there may be brain trauma involved, but that's our worry, and
we've got our nuts . . . as well as Peyton Manning!"

Oddly, this point of view has recently gained plenty of sympathetic admirers in more sophisticated circles: witness the
rise of "cracker chic" on cable TV food programs for southern

cuisine and craft bourbons, or television's glorifying of hunt-
ing, American "pickers," and the ancient way of life depicted
on the History Channel's *Swamp People* or the Learning Channel's *Trailer Park: Welcome to Myrtle Manor.* Or perhaps you
prefer *Glamour Belles, Lizard Lick Towing, Sweet Home Ala-
bama,* or Animal Planet's *Hillbilly Handfishin'.* And everyone should prefer the elemental charm of Dog the Bounty
Hunter!

Of course, all this is dependent on typecasting rural people,
especially in the South, and chortling at a safe distance as its
representatives perform a sordid white minstrelsy (minus the
talent for tap dancing). More to the point, this programming
dictates a Federalist understanding of the rural: the people of
the countryside are unlike us. They are crude and violent, if
sometimes good for a laugh. If they are poor, it is because that's
how they like it. (As far as their poverty is concerned, the People of the Law are perfectly happy to say, "It's their culture and
who are we to judge?") For us, their culture provides the benefit
of an occasional shot of Elijah Craig twenty-one-year-old single
barrel or a plate of blackened redfish and cheesy grits but not
much more (except for the occasional night out slumming with
the line dancers). This sort of media representation reinforces
the old Federalist idea that rural culture requires policing. Surprisingly, even the protagonists of the above programs seem to
accept the idea that their undertakings benefit from the supervision of governmental grown-ups. At the end of the day, they
confess, "I've made some bad choices in my life."

And on the whole we left-leaners couldn't agree more. It's their own fault! They need to take a good hard look *inside*!

Taken together, these characteristics create our *founding* national psychopathology. All the social issues that will lead debate in the next federal election cycle will be a reflection of this psychopathology, the "neurotic personality of our time," as Freud's student Karen Horney expressed it.

And a long time it has been.

THE ENDLESS BABBLE OF SELF-CREATION

Do the People of the Id do anything other than what everyone does? Don't we all turn the endless babble of self-creation, of loyalty to a particular world of ideas and things and narratives (the constellation of personality), into our own communal Categorical Imperative, our own sense of duty?

It doesn't help that liberals are always banging away in that annoying, self-righteous way of theirs: "Don't drive trucks, they're destroying the climate; in fact, don't even drive a car (never mind that I've got a BMW minivan—the kids!); mass transit is the way to go; don't fly off to Mexico for a vacation; in fact, don't fly, not even to see your mother stuck away in Tiny Town, Texas; you can Skype her; and if you must ride a motorcycle, wear a helmet; don't drink Coke or anything with corn syrup in it—you're killing your own children with that stuff!; speaking of killing your children, don't let the boys play football—what kind of parent are you?; what in the world do you

need an Uzi for anyway?; you don't see me with a gun, do you?;
don't water your lawn; own only one house, a small one with
net-zero energy (you *rent*? a *trailer*?); recycle your Budweiser
beer cans; how can you drink that piss water?; buy craft beers,
it aids the local economy; buy local, buy local!; buy your broc-
colini at the farmer's market on Saturday (you don't eat brocco-
lini? you're missing a real treat!); ride a bicycle; hire a life coach
and a personal trainer; you're fat, God are you fat, are you paying any attention at all?; learn to meditate; let's see, you already
stopped smoking, somehow, good for you; for God's sake, stop
eating meat; no to factory farming!; no to meat-packing plants!
no to Iowa!; we will allow you to eat bacon on occasion because
everybody eats bacon, especially bacon dipped in maple syrup;
even vegans eat bacon when no one is watching; do you really
need to hunt? it's that important to you?; join PETA; no to
fracking!; no hard drugs like heroin or meth, but a marijuana
gummy bear is okay should you travel to Colorado. But just
one, that shit is strong, not like the old days. Finally, read a
book. Have you *ever* read a book?"

To all of which the People of the Id reply, "This is not America!" and sometimes they say a good deal more. In November 2014, the Westminster, Massachusetts, Board of Health
proposed a ban on the sale of tobacco products in the town,
provoking a response so vitriolic that a public meeting of the
Board was closed after twenty minutes and the Board members
escorted from the building under police protection. As neighbors come and go at Vincent's Country Store, they feed on one

another's rage. Nate Johnson, an egg farmer, told *The New York Times*: "They're just taking away everyday freedoms, little by little." Deborah Hancock added that she was afraid to wear her cross: "I'm thinking, 'Am I going to be beheaded?'" "It's un-American," added Rick Sparrow, a house painter.

They're wrong about "un-American," not that that's a good thing. It's American, all too American. What they're thinking of as un-American is paternalism and inequality, also perfectly traditional American qualities. The owners of these qualities are urban, economically privileged, literate in hideously subtle ways, and well practiced in expressions of disdain. These qualities constitute, for the most part, my own point of view (loosely expressed). But it is also the point of view of what Max Weber called a "status group."

The people who are part of this status group are likely to be members of the upper and upper-middle classes and propertied in modest or immodest ways. They are likely to possess technical, managerial, and intellectual skills; these skills are a form of property—not physical property, but nonetheless property that the People of the Id do not have. They are likely to have secure employment, bright career prospects, and privileged benefits like health insurance and pensions. To share the viewpoint of this liberal status group—as, say, Rachel Maddow and her viewers do—is to belong to a group with a specific style of life that the group believes reflects *honor* on its members. Most troublesome, this status group fancies that it is superior to the hidebound rural illiterate, and as far as I can tell it *is* superior.

But that is little consolation when the illiterates band together against the haughtiness of this status group and take over the U.S. Senate in the midterm elections of 2014 because, count 'em, *there are a lot of rural states.*

A lot!

And as more and more of Tyler Cowen's machine economy drifts to concentrated population centers on the coasts, we learn that average is not over; it's simply been left behind in the thirty-six or so flyover states full of ill-educated, average folk living in something close to poverty and feeling really, really resentful. Why do white males in left-out areas of the country vote for Republicans? Bigotry is involved, for sure. But it's also true that at present some thirty million workers in their prime working years are "non-employed." They've fallen outside the labor market. (This does not include the workingman's last re-sort, disability, for which there is a large and largely fraudulent industry of lawyers and doctors, especially in Appalachia.) And the share of prime age men who are nonemployed has tripled since the 1960s from 5 percent to 16 percent. Whether it's fair or not, much of this gets blamed on Democrats.

The unintended consequence of what Cowen describes may be that the Senate will be dominated by these left-out states for decades to come. The population may be on the coasts, but North Dakota gets just as many senators as California (at long last the Federalists get bitten in the ass by their own aristocratic invention—the U.S. Senate). On the other hand, defeats like

2014 may baffle and infuriate the members of our liberal status group, the People of the Law, but at the end of the day they are still urban, literate, prosperous, and proudly liberal. So they click on the five-dollar donation for MoveOn.org's *crise-du-jour* and proceed with their interesting lives.

The People of the Id, on the other hand, are stuck. It doesn't matter that the election of Ted Cruz or Rand Paul feels to them like vengeance; Ted Cruz and Rand Paul are not going to help them. It doesn't matter if conservative governors like Scott Walker of Wisconsin strip public employee unions of their pensions and the right to organize; misery may love company, but that does not help the fact that there is nothing about the future of the American economy that includes the People of the Id. Tyler Cowen and Thomas Piketty are in agreement on that point. Their fate is still isolation, poverty, ignorance, and more than their proportionate share of self-destruction (crime, alcoholism, drugs, and domestic violence). That is certainly a sad thing for them, and it should be a bad thing for everyone.

Nevertheless, gun in hand, the People of the Id will stand up for themselves. They'll think they look like Charlton Heston holding a flintlock over his head, but they'll look like crazy, violent People of the Id to the rest of us. They will live in a teary-eyed wash of homemade virtues. But, then, whether liberal or conservative, everyone's virtues are homemade. They are forms of civic narcissism. One thing is for certain, this mortal impasse we suffer under, and have suffered under for over two

hundred years, will not yield to a simple moral division of good
from bad, or liberal from conservative, because, as Nietzsche
understood, it is more than anything else an expression of social Will to Power.

LAST STORIES

When a collective is willing to die for its narcissism—for its
stories—the result is inevitably fascistic (the Nazis were storytellers before they were a war machine) because stories "worth
dying for" are intolerant of other stories: they believe that their
story should be the *last* story. As Mussolini understood fascism,
it is the supremacy of the state and its nationalist legends. If you
do not agree with these legends and the power they confer on
the state, you cannot be allowed to taint the minds of the rest
of the good citizens. You must be killed or made invisible. The
People of the Id are acutely intolerant of stories other than their
own, and so is American capitalism.

The only story worth dying for is the story that says there are
no last stories. Unfortunately, those who are willing to die for
the idea that there are no last stories are usually spared the trouble—they are eliminated, removed from consideration through
violence, gulags, or market invisibility. As a blogger in Saudi
Arabia learned to his horror this year, "opening the conversation" regarding the meaning of Islam gets you exactly one thousand lashes delivered over ten years in prison. We're more subtle

here, of course. We need only find that certain ways of thinking (whether political or artistic) lack "commercial viability."

What is needed in order to confront "last stories" is exactly
what seems not to be possible. Cultures need to be able to recognize how destructive and self-destructive those convictions
can be, and then they need to find the imaginative capacity
and the generosity for new ideas, new forms of self-perception,
by which they can live less narcissistically and less destructively.
We live within the bastion of a community Ego. When that
Ego is challenged, we can react in two ways. We can defend
it in all the unending and destructive ways we know too well,
or we can abandon the bastion of the Ego and dance. Again,
Robert Aitken:

> [The dance] is the great joke of Zen. It is the great joke of the
> universe. There is no absolute at all, and that is the absolute.
> Enlightenment is practice . . . And what is practice? Getting
> on with it. When you defend, you are blocking the practice.
> When you dance, you are getting on with it.

Unfortunately, while the human capacity for self-
reinvention—for the dance—is accomplished only over centuries of messy struggle, the technological advances brought
upon *all* cultures in recent decades have moved at warp speed.
Our machines *accelerate* into a future that is humanly and en-
vironmentally bleak. I am not optimistic about the idea that
we will be able to dispose of our old, comfortable, vicious, and
infinitely varied "inherited stupidities," in large part because

politics—the means through which stories become social—
doesn't work at high velocity. As a consequence, what we have
now is not "politics" but "logistics." It is increasingly difficult
to imagine a place outside the administered space of techno-
capitalism and its self-congratulatory legends of intellectual
and commercial triumph. The Occupy Wall Street movement
occupied a literal place—Zuccotti Park—as well as a concep-
tual/narrative place, and for a moment much of our culture
paused, mesmerized by this odd spectacle, to wonder if there
were alternative ways of thinking about who we are and where
we're heading. The moment passed, but the gesture was important because, however briefly, it opened a space to the dance, to
play, and to *possibility*. The moment may have been ephemeral,
but it also showed us what is *essential* for the future. It revealed
a permanent need. It showed us the way to what Nietzsche
called, simply, "health."

In his bestselling *The Making of a Counter Culture*, from
1970, Theodore Roszak makes a similar point:

> But from my own point of view, the counter culture, far
> more than merely "meriting" attention, desperately re-
> quires it, since I am at a loss to know where, besides among
> these dissenting young people and their heirs of the next
> few generations, the radical discontent and innovation
> can be found that might transform this disoriented civili-
> zation of ours into something a human being can identify
> as home . . . The capacity of our emerging technocratic
> paradise to denature the imagination by appropriating to
> itself the whole meaning of Reason, Reality, Progress, and

Knowledge will render it impossible for men to give any name to their bothersomely unfulfilled potentialities but that of madness.

This was written almost thirty years before the founding of Google and the "technocratic paradise" that we live in today.

Work like Roszak's is now almost universally scorned and made to parade before the townsfolk with a large paisley H-for-Hippie sewn onto its jacket. But Roszak was only one of many intellectuals of the moment—including Herbert Marcuse, Paul Goodman, Alan Watt, Norman O. Brown, Marshall McLuhan, and a little later, George W. S. Trow—who together helped to lead a living opposition to technocracy. Through them, philosophy engaged social criticism, which engaged social activism and led to the invention of alternative ideas about how we should live. It was the last time that, in Paul Ricoeur's terms, we had both consonance and dissonance, both ideology and utopia as active principles in our culture. It was the last time our culture had some degree of health.

The worst thing we can do now is what we're doing: we forbid new stories. We forbid stories that run counter to our failing convictions, and we forbid stories that seek counter-worlds. And yet pursuing those stories may be the most radical, the most compassionate, and the most life-giving thing we can do in the present moment. Let's see from what Western traditions those stories derive their strength and what they might look like now and in the future. They might not be so strange. In fact, they may be no more difficult to adopt than a new set of clothes.

As Thomas Carlyle expressed it, perhaps all we need is a new tailor.

•

> The solution to the Romantic problem lies not in attempting the impossible, not in trying to stabilize the Self, but in continuous self-transformation, in continuously transcending tragedy, and comedy, and good, and evil. The Self is the rainbow, an illusion made up of ever changing substance, which hovers above the cataract of the tears of things. It is an illusion, but compared to it, the world we know is but the illusion of an illusion. With Nietzsche, Romanticism got to the root of its problem and found a stable solution to its difficulty in instability itself, in conceiving of life as the eternal possibility for continuous self-transformation.
>
> —MORSE PECKHAM

Part Two
SOMETHING WORTH BEING LOYAL TO

Let us all learn from stupidity.　　　　—MONTAIGNE

Hope, the forgivable madness.　　—ROBERT COOVER

What is it that we inherit when we "inherit stupidity"? Primarily, we inherit stories. These stories may be personally destructive and generally catastrophic, yet to stand opposed to them requires brave people. In the present moment, the most powerful stories contribute to the ever accelerating dehumanizing and dematerializing of our lifeworld, on the one hand, and the general collapse of the natural world, on the other. Of course, the two are related: if there is environmental collapse, the velocity of technological change will be responsible.

Like characters in Greek tragedy, we seem fated to push technology toward its ultimate degree as if we were possessed by malignant gods. We call these gods "curiosity" and "creativity" and "reason" and "progress," but when these words are perverted by technocrats, they are more like the four horsemen of the apocalypse. The technocrats explain that if they employ these qualities it is because they are what make us human. "Not to use our powers of curiosity and invention would be to deny our humanity!" So back we go to R & D for more of the same.

Meanwhile, "the Earth dies screaming," as Tom Waits put it, while we go on dreaming of electric sheep.

In spite of destruction past and future, the status quo urges us to remain hopeful that we can continue living through our inherited stupidities without driving ourselves to extinction. We are instructed to be hopeful nearly as often as we are instructed by researchers in the Happiness Industry to be happy. But what reason do the citizens of São Paulo have to be either happy or hopeful? A major industrial city of eleven million people, São Paulo is presently rationing water due to a shortage linked to environmental degradation and drought. Will it be the first major population center to collapse from climate change? Or will it be Los Angeles and the San Joaquin Valley?

For technocrats, hope usually takes this form: "Technology may be the source of the problem, but it will also be the source of the solution." Hope of that kind merely doubles down on technocratic madness: doing the same things and expecting different results. If we are to hope, we should employ a hope that is, as Robert Coover put it in his 1964 novel *The Origin of the Brunists*, a "forgivable madness." This is not hope that the rumors of ruin will not come true because our machines can be adjusted and infinitely tweaked. It is the hope that we can leave the old murderous stories behind and inhabit new stories. But in a world where people are joined to their stories as if to their own viscera, the idea that masses of people could be persuaded to leave their stories for new ones would seem to be lunacy.

And yet in a very real sense, many of us *are* leaving the stories we were born into and committing ourselves to the creation of new stories, new cultures, and new human relations to the universe. The rapid spread of Western Buddhism is one example, and it is everywhere around us, although it is not at what the geeks like to call a "tipping point." But we don't need to become Buddhists in order to find alternative stories to live through. We have our own countercultural traditions that work through art (and alongside groups dedicated to progressive social reform). All art is propositional: here is a world that you might inhabit—this music, this painting, this poem—although more often than not the work only reproduces the world we already inhabit. But, as Ricoeur has shown, that's ideology and not art. The last sections of this book will be devoted to clarifying the dissident/utopic tradition of the arts since Romanticism's first gestures of refusal and self-creation, and I will try to show how that tradition can be extended into the future (assuming we are to have one).

The idea that the "hope" for a world of new stories will save us from the robots or from climate collapse is, I admit, improbable in the extreme. And yet it is what needs to happen. We should liberate science and technology in their purist forms from those stories that claim that our well-being is dependent upon science working through the "military-corporate complex," to rephrase Dwight Eisenhower's famous warning. At the very least, advocates for science and technology need to take more responsibility for the real-world consequences of their work. They need to become morally intelligent. At present, they are not.

It may seem pitifully insufficient, but my hope is that we can create narratives that suggest counter-worlds in which we could live more knowingly, more honestly, and less destructively. We might even hope that the STEM-inclined would join us there in the spirit of play and creativity, rather than in the name of profit and self-aggrandizement. If that hope is madness, it is a madness we should be forgiven.

THE STRANGENESS OF BEAUTY

If the purpose of ideology is to make certain ideas and aesthetic forms familiar and therefore "normal," the purpose of art is to make the same forms strange. As Baudelaire put it, "the beautiful is always strange."

Although that may sound like mere iconoclasm, it is first and foremost a social judgment. The Russian formalist critic Viktor Shklovsky built his criticism around the idea that art defamiliarizes or "enstranges" the familiar world of habit and custom. As he writes in *Energy of Delusion*: "We shake hands on parting, as we know. We are used to it. We don't remember why we do this." The handshake is part of a story we have forgotten. It is part of a world of what the critic Morse Peckham called "reigning platitudes." It is a "natural"-feeling thing to do, but that naturalness is an illusion. Art makes us feel the strangeness of a handshake.

Art's strategy is to undermine those stories that seem so matter-of-fact by revealing their arbitrariness. And what is arbitrary is open to re-arbitration, to negotiation. When Jimi Hendrix encouraged us to "get experienced," he was thinking of how music, psychedelic-ecstatic clothing, and, of course, drugs tend to enstrange our familiar routines, unmasking the world where "white-collar conservatives flash down the street" and point their plastic fingers. Once unmasked, we are free to let our "freak flag fly." Enstrangement and the freedom it restores are inherently inimical to social stability, a fact that bourgeois culture has never been slow to recognize.*

When art works in this way, it is participating in what Peck-ham called "human history's second chapter." The first chap-ter was the establishment of cities/civilization in which social roles were rigidly defined and replicated from generation to generation. As recently as the nineteenth century, young men like Percy Bysshe Shelley had severely limited choices for what social roles they could take up. If one was the first-born son (and Shelley was), he would become lord of the manor, man-ager of rents, and member of the House of Lords if there was a family "seat" (Shelley's father was a member of parliament). If that wasn't the case, then a young man of property could attend school and then enter either the military or the clergy (although he was not a man of property, Coleridge had just begun a career in the clergy when he was spared that fate by an annuity from Josiah Wedgwood). Science was still a gentleman's avocation, a

---

* Which is probably why you can now buy a Jimi Hendrix postage stamp.

hobby, and not a serious social role, and to claim the role of poet was beyond the pale. Shelley's determination to be a poet and not the Second Baronet of Castle Goring was thus a new form of social revolt, a fact that was lost on no one, especially his father. Needless to say, it was even worse for women and those born into the "lower orders." But since the Romantics, Peckham argues, we have had a tradition—and a second chapter—that does not accept the necessity of defined roles and does not accept the necessity of the social world into which we just happen to have been born. In short, art became the way in which the disaffected refused to take a place in the reigning social order.*

In literature, understanding this second chapter requires going back beyond the Romantics to Rabelais and the novelist Laurence Sterne in order to discover the source of Romanticism's Ethics of Play. It was in literature that the countercultural impulse was first most fully developed, although painting and music were not far behind.

VAIHINGER'S CHILDREN

For the Russian critic Mikhail Bakhtin, Rabelais's *Gargantua and Pantagruel* was the supreme example of the "carnivalesque." Like medieval Carnival, in which for the duration

---

* Interestingly, Isaac Newton fits this model, too. In his youth, Newton was expected to take over the family farm (his father had died when he was a child). He expressed his dislike of farming by letting the cattle wander wherever they liked. Shortly thereafter, he was allowed to return to school, where he continued his study of mathematics.

of the festival people were allowed to mock the official my-thologies of the state, the carnivalesque in literature is anarchic. It doesn't stop with mocking social structures; it mocks the substratum on which society sits: it mocks reality as such. In the carnivalesque, reality is another word for disenchantment, and it is the artist's job to enchant the world anew, employing any means available. Artists destroy the familiar and open the world to infinite possibility and to *play*. Through laughter, they ridicule official fictions, enliven the utopic impulse, and make available the courage to live differently.

What stands opposite Rabelaisian play is mimesis. While there are many ways of understanding mimesis, it is at heart an expression of confidence in the idea that the order of language can adequately represent the order of nature, es-pecially the everyday life of human beings. Even a writer as apparently fanciful as Dante—who peopled the *Inferno* with real, fictional, and mythological characters as if there were no differences among them—insisted on the sufficiency of language to provide the truth about reality. He feared that without the assumption of the adequacy of language, poetry could not do the essential work of justifying God's order. His *stil novo* (the "new style" that used vernacular Italian rather than Latin) could be *dolce* (sweet) but it also had a job to do.

Dante developed a motif that first appeared in his early semi-autobiographical poem, *The Vita Nuova*: the poet is only a scribe who copies from the "book of memory." Thus, there is final parity (according to Dante's fiction) between thing experienced, thing remembered, and thing related through the book. In this sense, in the *Inferno* Dante-the-poet is merely Virgil's scribe, and what Virgil reveals to him comes from a source so worthy (God) that there is no room for doubt. Dante may stand at two removes from the Divine Idea but there is no suggestion that his poem is in any important sense a distortion of the Idea. (Like his contemporary St. Thomas Aquinas, Dante's theology was Aristotelian in orientation. It is a cause-effect theology.) When Francesca tells her story of being ruined by love for Paolo, her presence, her voice, and her story are meant to resonate with authenticity and justice. Dante attempts to banish irony and banish the idea that his story could be told differently. From first to last, what the poet inscribes is a statement of truth: *thus it is.* For Dante, the function of both book and world is *to refer* to the justice of our place in the world, and the justice of the world itself, all guaranteed by the only thing that can escape language, God himself.

That's Dante's presiding fiction.

But if memory is a book in Dante, it is a "bag" in Rabelais (the young Gargantua refers to "*la gibbesiere* [pouch or bag] *de ma memoire*" in his famous catalogue of ass wipes). Out of this bag comes not the orderliness of the mimetic text (with its beginning and end, hero and villain, faithful representations of "things") but the inexhaustible catalogues of verbal artifacts that function as the Rabelaisian "world." It was in Rabelais that the West first dared to imagine that the cosmos is made

of language as well as of things, of mind as well as of matter.*
As with Einstein's spacetime, Rabelais discovered mindmatter.

Worst of all for a mind like Dante's, the implication of Rabelais's fiction is that *everything* is open to reordering, everything is carried before the energy of the artist's freedom, even
God's order. In spite of the threat of excommunication coming from the Franciscan academics at the Sorbonne, Rabelais's
faith was in the mind's profane freedom to undo all of the care-
ful little fables of the official world of church and state. Dante
would probably have dropped Rabelais into a *bolgia* in the sixth
circle of hell with the other heretics. (Dante: there is a divine
order and it is just; Rabelais: there is no order at all and that is
a joy.)

Francois Rabelais was not an anomaly. He is part of a tradition
in the arts that survives to this day. But whereas literary realism has its Great Tradition of the novel to point to, stretching
from Jane Austen through Henry James, Hemingway, Norman
Mailer, and Saul Bellow to the present, the Other Tradition is
not much known to us, although Steven Moore's recent *The
Novel: An Alternative History* goes to great lengths (seven hundred pages) to correct this lack. Even at that length Moore gets

---

* It is not just memory that is a bag but language itself. As Nietzsche observed, every word
is a bag: every word "is a pocket into which now this, now that, now several things at once
have been put!" (316)

only to the year 1600 and so just barely reaches the period I'm discussing. The important thing to see is not only the recondite fact that this tradition exists but that it is still among us in 2015. It is important to my argument to acknowledge this tradition and to emerge in the present knowing that *Rabelais lives!* In fact, I would call the Rabelaisian tradition a *lineage*. Like Buddhist dharma, it represents a sort of wisdom literature in the West whose responsibility it is to reveal the delusion that words have some sort of durable relationship to Reality. This lineage frees us from those delusions and opens up the world to possibility. It is truly an aspect of enlightenment.

The best known Rabelaisian in English literature is Laurence Sterne. Rabelais was Sterne's favorite author (along with the earlier Boccaccio (1313-1375) and Cervantes (1548-1616)), and Sterne refers to him often in his self-absorbed masterpiece *Tristram Shandy*. What Sterne loved in Rabelais is self-evident in *Shandy*: the fun of making things up, linking them, making a coherent if iconoclastic world—a "hobbyhorse" world—whose only identity is that it is everything that that other world, the official one, is not. For Sterne the idea that language is in some sense a mirror held to nature was so laughable that the only criticism he allowed himself was . . . *laughter*. Instead, Sterne called the novel the art of digression, an imitation of the infinite openness and play of language and of nature, a proposition that he took the trouble to diagram for his reader in gleeful satire of Aristotle's "unity of action":

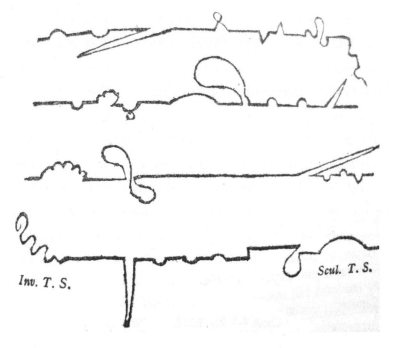

Inv. T. S.   *Scul. T. S.*

Sterne made his anarchistic intentions clear in the first pages of the novel stating, "in writing what I have set about, I shall confine myself neither to [Horace's] rules, nor to any man's rules that ever lived." As we will see, Sterne's literary anarchism had a deep influence on, of all things, Romanticism.

STERNE TO DENIS DIDEROT (1713–1784)

Diderot actually met Sterne in Paris during the trip that would provide the material for Sterne's last work, *A Sentimental Journey*. Diderot once said of *Shandy*, "This book, so mad, so wise, so gay [is] the Rabelais of the English." Diderot's homage to

Sterne, *Jacques the Fatalist* (not available to English readers until 1959) is a profoundly Shandean novel. In fact, it includes "playgiarized" passages from *Shandy*. These playgiarisms bookend his own inventions and comic circumlocutions.

Jacques is a novel in the *picaresque* tradition and concerns a Master and Jacques, his servant, during a long journey by horse (for what purpose is never clear because it doesn't matter; as in Chuck Berry's song, the story has no particular place to go). It happens that Jacques is something of a philosopher who advocates an extreme form of determinism. He believes that everything that happens must happen because it has been "written up yonder," not by God but through the idea that once the material world is set in motion everything that follows follows of necessity. Through Jacques, Diderot satirizes some of the more extreme versions of mechanical materialism. To a degree, he lampoons himself and his *philosophe* colleagues like Voltaire; both were tempted to believe that everything is the result of the peculiar organization of matter in the universe: once the material universe is set and put in motion, the future is inevitable. The means of this lampooning is the playful texture of the novel's arch and comic rhetoric.

> How had they met? By chance, like everyone else.* What were their names? What does it matter to you? Whence had they come? From the nearest possible spot. Where were they going? Do we ever know where we're going? What were they saying? The master said nothing and Jacques said that his

---

* Everything happens by chance: unlike Jacques, Diderot himself was no Fatalist.

captain said that everything that happens to us down here, good or bad, was written up yonder.

Diderot was aware of the literary lineage he took part in. His recipe for novel writing was this: "Take . . . four chapters of Don Quixote; a well-chosen paragraph of Rabelais; mix all this with a reasonable quantity of *Jacques the Fatalist* . . . and change these drugs as herbs are varied by substituting others possessing somewhat the same qualities."

DIDEROT TO GOETHE (1749–1832)

While Goethe's *Faust I* is a relatively straightforward tragic drama, *Faust II* is *weird*. It is a recursive, hallucinatory anti-novel featuring at one point a character who is, somehow, a homunculus in a glass phial (a nod, perhaps, to Sterne's bewildered homunculus—making its way from father Walter to mother Elizabeth—whose unhappy chore it is to become Tristram). This homunculus traipses about, up and down stairs, discoursing grandly from the shelter of his phial.

Similarly, while *Wilhelm Meister's Apprenticeship* is elaborate, it is tame in comparison with the later work, *Wilhelm Meister's Travels. Meister II* is a rich Shandean blend of narratives, digressions within digressions, and magnificent if inconclusive stories in a *picaresque* style. Although Goethe knew of Sterne's work and called him "the most beautiful spirit that ever lived," much of the Sterne influence came to Goethe indirectly, through Diderot. Goethe had read, translated, and delighted in *Jacques the Fatalist* even before it was known in France.

> From six o'clock until past noon I have read *Jacques the Fatal-ist* without interruption. I read it with the delight of the Bel of Babel enjoying an immense feast, and thank God I was able to devour such a portion with the greatest appetite, all at once, as if I were drinking a glass of water, and yet with indescribable voluptuousness.

A century later, the man whom Morse Peckham called the "triumph of Romanticism," Friedrich Nietzsche, was still echoing Goethe's enthusiasm for Sterne, whose "squirrel-soul leaped restlessly from branch to branch":

> How in a book for free spirits, should there be no mention of Laurence Sterne, whom Goethe honoured as the most liberated spirit of his century! Let us content ourselves here simply with calling him the most liberated spirit of all time, in comparison with whom all others seem stiff, square, intolerant and boorishly direct.

GOETHE TO SCHILLER (1759–1805) AND SCHLEGEL (1772–1829)

Goethe's close friend Friedrich Schiller was the first to formalize the aesthetic that begins with Rabelais under the rubric of "play" (he also refers often to Sterne's *Shandy*). He was the first to understand the social and political implications of play.

Schiller's logic went something like this: nature displays itself
to us as infinite play (nature is always in the process of becoming; organic nature is, after all, driven by mutation and chance).
As part of nature, humans ought also to be playful and self-
creative, and to participate in nature's lusty self-becoming.
Tragically, humans find themselves enslaved to work, to machines, and to "perverse and brutal" social authority. Works
of art are a protest against industrialism's unnatural use of humans, trapping them in one-dimensional lives. For Schiller,
art expresses our grievance with the machine world while at
the same time showing the way forward. Art is both critique
and cure. The artist is an exile, she is alien, she is deliberately
"untimely," as Nietzsche put it. The beauty of art is the promise of happiness Schiller makes to his audience: "every object
of natural beauty outside me carries a guarantee of happiness
which calls to me: be free like me."

What was most important about Schiller's aesthetic thinking was that it departed from the idea (a misreading of Aristotle) that art is the imitation of nature understood as something
individual, fixed, and dead. Rather, Schiller suggested that art
participates in nature's freedom, a freedom that moves through
nature as an organic whole.

This suggestion prepared German philosophy and art for
Romanticism. Its effect was still being felt at the end of the
century in Vaihinger and Nietzsche. It was to Schiller's ethic of
freedom/play that Vaihinger traced his philosophy of As-If: "I

understood his theory of play as the primary element of artistic creation and enjoyment; and it had great influence on the development of my thought, for later on I recognized in play the 'As if,' as the driving force of aesthetic activity and intuition."

The importance of Schiller to the next century of ideas cannot be overstated. Almost singlehanded, he turned the development of Romanticism from Rousseau's idea—that we ought to return to the primitive state of nature—to the idea that the full realization of our nature is something that develops over time. Our nature is a destination and not an origin. Even Karl Marx, sounding very much the Marxist Romantic he was in 1844, wrote that "life itself only appears as the *means to life*." This is why all of the fatalist bromides about "human nature" are so false and destructive. We're often told that we are violent by nature, possessive by nature, monogamous, polygamous, nurturing, or selfish, all "by nature." Human nature as something fixed and eternal merely apologizes for brutality.

But for the Romantics, our only nature is to summon our nature in and through an analogue world that is the creation of that unknown thing that we call imagination. Romanticism "degodded Nature," in Schiller's phrase, meaning that it rid it not only of deities but also of the idols that followed the death of the gods. These idols are the consequence of looking at nature as something that stands independently outside of our attention.

The empirical gaze creates idols, as does the worshipful gaze of bad nature poetry and painting. For example, a rainbow is not simply a refraction of light in water, and it is not simply this beautiful thing upon which we look with reverential awe while praising its "beauty." It is the creation of the physiology of our eyes (we see what light our eyes allow us to see, a narrow band on the electromagnetic spectrum), and it is the creation of our narratives about rainbows, especially our stories about their beauty.

Consider the work of the painter J. W. Turner in paintings like *Slave Ship*. For Turner, light was not this thing in the distance to be studied as "visually perceived radiant energy," nor was it a crudely romantic abandonment of self to the authority of that great idol "the beauty of nature." Turner understood himself to be the creator of these lights, colors, and swirling motions; the *Slave Ship* has very little to do with a ship (which can only be vaguely seen) and a lot to do with the painting as an *expression* of an intuition that is Turner's own. It doesn't imitate nature, it creates it.

Schiller not only opened the way for Romanticism, he also provided a model for what would come to be known as the dialectic, first fully elaborated by Hegel and Marx, Hegel's querulous heir. It is not too much to say that in a few powerful essays—especially "The Aesthetic Education of Man," and "Of Naïve and Sentimental Poetry"—Schiller revealed the intellectual path for *both Romanticism and socialism*. In more familiar terms, Schiller is at the origin of two forms of political action that are still very much with us *in potentia*: counterculture and revolution.

In spite of a feud over a review Schiller wrote of a book of poetry by one of Schlegel's friends, Schiller was an important influence on Friedrich Schlegel. Along with his brother Auguste, Schlegel published the famous Romantic journal *Athenäum* through which the two developed the early philosophy of Romanticism (he was the first to use this word to describe a new school of thought and art). Unfortunately, his career is divided by an early commitment to play and a later unpalatable enthusiasm for medieval Catholicism. He concluded by editing the right-wing Catholic journal *Concordia* in which he critiqued the very ideas he had advanced as a younger man. Fortunately, we are free to choose between Schlegel's versions of himself, just as we must with Hegel (the youthful Hegel of *The Phenomenology of Spirit* is very different from old man Hegel in *The Philosophy of Right*). And the young Schlegel shared and developed Schiller's love for Sterne and Diderot.

> In case you cannot deny some sympathy with Sterne's sensibility, I am sending you a book, but I have to warn you about it so that you will be careful with regard to strangers, for it has the fortune or misfortune to be somewhat notorious. It is Diderot's *The Fatalist*.

Like Schiller, Schlegel embraced the idea that art should participate in nature's infinite development.

The Romantic kind of poetry is still in the state of becoming; that, in fact, is its real essence: that it should forever be
becoming and never perfected . . . It alone is infinite, just as
it alone is free; and it recognizes as its first commandment
that the will of the poet can recognize no law above itself.*

THE ROMANTIC TRADITION (1825–PRESENT)

From this point forward, art as a dissident social force was central to European culture. The story of art after Romanticism is
almost exclusively the story of the refusal of bourgeois norms
and expectations in the name of the unruly freedom of the artist who refuses his bourgeois job description as entertainer and
imitator of what is said to be real ("Make It New," said Ezra
Pound). This tendency was famously present among the English
Romantic poets. For example, in his epic satire *Don Juan* Byron
mostly forgets that his story is supposed to be about a sexual
predator and becomes yet another Shandean wonder of inexhaustible digressions. Byron was the least "customary" of poets.
The ethics of play was also present in Thomas Carlyle's "philosophy of clothes" in *Sartor Resartus*. Carlyle announces trium-
phantly that philosophy is "a continual battle against Custom;
an ever-renewed effort to *transcend* the sphere of blind Custom,
and so become Transcendental." For Carlyle as for Nietzsche,
philosophy is the ongoing battle against inherited stupidity.

---

* Compare Schlegel's remark to the comment by Robert Aitken on the importance of
Buddhist "dance."

The next generation of Romantic artists made it even clearer that their work was not about nature mysticism or a love of the medieval so much as it was about the continuation of a social struggle. This is emphatically, even violently the case with Richard Wagner. It is not much known, but Wagner was an enthusiastic observer of the revolutions of 1848 and a participant in the Dresden uprising of 1849. One of his friends during this period was the anarchist Mikhael Bakunin with whom he helped organize the barricades against the Prussian army. By legend, Wagner also paid for the manufacture of grenades and oversaw the destruction of his own opera house (a self-serving gesture, we are told, because he didn't think it was worthy of his talents).

In his essay "Art and Revolution" Wagner wrote, "True Art is revolutionary because its very existence is opposed to the ruling spirit of the community." Sounding very much like a socialist Romantic, he wrote in the same essay:

> From the dishonouring slave-yoke of the universal journey-
> manhood, with its sickly Money-soul, we wish to soar to
> the free manhood of Art, with the star-rays of its World-
> soul. [Wow!]

Wagner was sympathetic to socialist causes as early as the anarchic *Tannhäuser* (first written in Dresden) and as late as the composition of *Das Rheingold*, in which the malignant dwarf Alberich in his frenzy for gold enslaves the Niebelungen in a subterranean "Satanic mill."

But what made Wagner and Wagnerism socially powerful

was the titanic originality of the operas themselves, Wagner's god-like ability to create a world that was clearer, more dignified, and more passionate than the world itself. For his admirers, the world of Wagner's *Ring of the Niebelungen* was better, was better conceived, than the real world, which could only look tawdry and hopeless in comparison. Most significantly, Wagner's work led to the self-identification of thousands of the most adventuresome minds of Europe (Nietzsche and Baudelaire chief among them) as *Wagnerians*. Not German, not French: Wagnerian. To be Wagnerian was, in Goethe's phrase, an "elective affinity" not restricted by the social structures of the past. Even though Wagner's art moved through ancient Nordic myth, his eye was always on the future. His essay "The Artwork of the Future" was a description of the relationship of the arts— drama, poetry, and music—in a perfect synthesis with the *volk*, the people who would inhabit a world where such artwork was possible. His worldview was not medieval; it was utopian.

The Wagnerians were followed by Symbolism, which the great literary critic Edmund Wilson claimed was related to Romanticism as the "second flood of the same tide." And Symbolism, as Wilson notes, was still playing itself out as late as the 1930s in Yeats, Eliot, and Joyce, and the icons of twentieth-century art— Picasso, Mondrian, and Kandinsky—all of whom had early symbolist periods before moving into cubism and abstract art.

Symbolism was followed by Impressionism, Expressionism, then Dada, Surrealism, and the rest of the unholy family of modernist "–isms" and their attendant literary geniuses from

Virginia Wolff, to Gertrude Stein, Djuna Barnes, Joyce, Beckett, Flann O'Brien, and onward to John Barth, Gilbert Sorrentino, and Ann Quinn. This tradition lives on to this day, even if it is presently somewhat chastened and beaten about the ears. But as recently as 1964 that most playful American genius Donald Barthelme could write, "Play is one of the great possibilities of art; it is also . . . the eros principle whose repression means total calamity." Humorless practitioners of the novel of "sovereign fact" produce such calamities regularly. These native worshippers of fact (on the Wolfe/Franzen axis) seek the traditional virtues of the realist novel but fail as "the result of a lack of seriousness."

Of course, in that same year, 1964, the youth of the West began falling in love with play once again, much to the consternation of the formerly robust taletellers of national honor, domino theories, *Leave It to Beaver* idylls, and the saga of the commie menace. And so from the Haight to the Village to London and Paris and far-flung outposts in India and Tibet, "imagination is taking power," as some sidewalk prophet scrawled in a stairwell of the Sorbonne in May 1968.

Margaret Thatcher once said of capitalist economics, "There is no alternative." She could just as plausibly have said the same thing about the pleasures of capitalist culture whose entertainments and enthusiasms saturate Western society. And yet where there is art, there is always an alternative. Art creates dissatisfaction with things as they are, it creates a yearning for something different, and it provides ideas about what that something different might feel like. This was gospel for the English Romantics, especially the young Wordsworth, and it is gospel even now especially among indie rockers and musicians (a point I will elaborate shortly), less so among writers (a point I have already elaborated).

So, what appeared to be mere personal eccentricity in Rabelais and Sterne—artist eccentrics bored with the straight face of authority, riding their hobbyhorses roughshod over custom— became with the Romantics a profound and at times dangerous social movement that has spread its wings out over us for the last 220 years. It is in this way that the Idea (as Hegel called it) works its way forward, looking for its opportunities, prodded by despair, embarrassed by its own failures, but never dead. And how could it ever be dead? It is the force of life itself, life's Spirit.

THE CRAZY WISDOM OF LARS VON TRIER'S *MELANCHOLIA*

As I have suggested, our culture believes that truth resides with scientific empiricism, even in areas that would seem to be well outside of science. As we've seen, if Buddhist meditation is to be broadly adopted, then the boys in the white lab coats must first put the Good Science Seal of Approval on it. Hence comes Sam Harris's scientistic notion of a "Buddhism without religion," Google's techno-Buddha, and the use of Buddhism as a means of branding any kind of god-awful consumer crap. But there is still the presence of a Not-Bot in our culture, an anti-bot whose tradition begins with Romanticism and whose present is, as it has always been, in the arts. This is especially the case when the art has the wisdom to resist a culture that seems to want *everything* to be filtered by Big Data and its algorithms before spilling out as consumer products. One critically reviled but lucid and, I think, finally beautiful example of the presence of the Romantic Not-Bot is Lars von Trier's cosmos-embracing *Melancholia*, from 2011.

Melancholia announces its Romantic intentions immediately. The title itself claims a place alongside the great romantic spiritual laments, like Coleridge's "Dejection: an Ode," Shelley's "Stanzas: Written in Dejection, Near Naples," and Keats's great "Ode to Melancholy." But the film's true romantic touchstone is a little later in time: the film opens with the ethereal gloom of the overture to Wagner's *Tristan und Isolde*.

There is, I suppose, a plot in this film, although (as in most opera) it is unsubtle and mostly a frame for supporting other purposes. There are two ground situations, both in the same location: a mansion on a large estate with, as we are reminded by the proud owner (John, played by Kiefer Sutherland), an eighteen-hole golf course.

The first situation is a lavish wedding reception that is gradually but completely destroyed (and the marriage with it) from the bottom up, as if its foundation were eroded from beneath by waves. The problem is that the conventional rituals of love, marriage, and celebration cannot withstand the bipolar realism of the family of the bride (Justine, played by Kirsten Dunst). Her manic father Max (John Hurt) explodes the idea of monogamous fidelity by picking up two women guests— both of whom, he claims, are named Betty. The Pan-like Max cavorts like a goat among women who have no identity at all. He seems to ask, "What is there in women to be faithful to? They're all just Bettys."

Justine's mother Gaby (Charlotte Rampling) is the depressive end of this bipolar family. Her destruction of the illusions of marriage and romantic love is most unsubtle. She represents the brutal realism of the depressed person, the ultimate realism. She seems to say, essentially, "Why are you allowing yourself to assume the stupid role of blushing bride in this preposterous ritual with these deluded people? I know you see as I do. So, why don't you admit it and leave? If you stay, this evening may be pleasant, but in the long run the delusions will come to the fore and everyone will suffer. But worst of all, you will be guilty of dishonesty."

Of course, the "normal" people at the party have their own unwitting role to play in this twilight of the idols. John is constantly reminding people about how much money this party is costing him, as if the wedding were not much different from his golf course, a mere status statement. In this, John has much in common with Justine's employer, Jack (Stellan Skarsgard). They are both "hungry ghosts," people lost to money and materialism. Jack is surely the most unpleasant character in the movie, even if he is an operatic overstatement of the hollow, heartless capitalist.

Even the groom, Michael (Alexander Skarsgard), contributes to the demolition. When he is asked to make a speech to his bride, he fumbles the opportunity as if struck with stage fright, or as if it had never occurred to him to wonder why he wanted to marry Justine, beyond the bounty of her breasts, of course. When he finally manages to say something, what he says is either vulgar ("I never thought I'd marry someone so gorgeous") or hopelessly trite ("I'm the luckiest man in the world"). As the camera turns to Justine, her hopeful smile at the beginning of Michael's speech slowly dissolves until it is nothing less than the end of all illusions. Michael is not giving her any evidence that her mother is wrong. Or her father: Michael's impatience to get the rigmarole of the wedding over with so that he can have free access to Justine's body suggests that he is not entirely unlike Max.*

The second situation, and the second half of the film, concerns the approach of a "rogue" planet on a collision course with the Earth. Because the two have already been shown colliding in the film's "overture," there is not much suspense. The audience knows what's coming. What the audience may not

* Someone has access to Justine's body that night, but it isn't the groom. Instead, she balls a party guest in one of John's sand traps. The fact that this went down in a sand trap would seem over the top except that the famous conclusion of Michelangelo Antonioni's *La Notte* (1961) ends with Giovanni (Marcello Mastroianni) raping his wife (Jeanne Moreau) in a sand trap on a private golf course owned by a Milan billionaire. Both *Melancholia* and *La Notte* feature lavish parties full of selfish, superficial people on the grounds of wealthy capitalists who imagine themselves to be eminent because of money; both films also feature leading characters (Moreau, Dunst) who see through the self-satisfaction of wealth because of their suicidal depression. The depressed person is the ultimate realist.

understand is that the world—the world of human conventions—has already been destroyed in the apocalypse of the
wedding.

All the nice, comforting social fictions of marriage, status,
and career have been bitterly laughed into oblivion. The contrast between the deluded hypocrisies of how we'd like life to
be and the grim honesty of the depressive's view of how things
really are does not condemn the film's characters but ridicules
them. They are not evil. They are a fragile tissue of preposterous fictions. They are ludicrous. They are afraid, like children,
of the truth. Their childishness makes them ridiculous. For example, when Justine's sister Claire (played by the *uber*-brilliant
Charlotte Gainsbourg) suggests that they experience the end
of the world on the terrace, embracing, and drinking a glass of
wine (the '48 Lafite Rothschild, one hopes), Justine replies that
her idea is a "piece . . . of . . . shit."

Yet another world destroyed by the film is the world of
Hollywood conventions. In *Melancholia*, there are no major
world cities in flames, no frantic media reports, no panic, no
anguished politicians, and no nuclear missiles launched into
space. This catastrophe happens not on a world stage but in the
eyes of the characters. Von Trier's confidence that the transition
from illusion to understanding can happen in his actor's eyes is
rewarded in scenes that are microscopically complex and emotionally visceral. Every major character, even the stolid John,
experiences this movement from hopeful illusion (in his case,
science's fantasy of mastery over a world of objects) to realist

acknowledgment. John repeatedly dismisses Claire's anxiety about the planet by claiming that astronomers have run the numbers and they're sure that the planet will miss Earth. Once he realizes that the numbers were wrong, he loses composure, takes all of the cyanide intended for Claire and their child as well, and runs off to commit suicide in the stables with a horse. (!) A good part of von Trier's point here would seem to be that mathematics does little to prepare us for the really Real, but in some way, depression does.

For Michael, his eyes must acknowledge that, first, he's not going to consummate the wedding that night, and, second, that his fantasy of married life (with poor Justine living under fruitful apple trees, for God's sake) is not going to happen either. (Pluck an apple, pluck a breast, ah!, the good life.) Claire must accept that her expectation of domestic felicity will not last, that all her carefully measured homeliness, especially her fantasies of her son's growing up, are not going to happen. Jack, too, has a transition, even if it is one of angry denial. Justine tells her employer exactly what she thinks of him (she "hates" him), but she's only telling him what he already knows. What infuriates him is that someone actually said so to his face. He jumps in his car and runs away from this moment of recognition, tires squealing. The only major character who doesn't experience this transition is Justine's mother because . . . she's already there! Her disappointments with Max provided her with reason for this transition a long time ago.

The last eye we see, the great Cyclops eye of the death planet

itself, is, like Yeats's sphinx, blank and pitiless. It knows nothing. It simply is what is. It is both Nietzsche's twilight of the
idols (putting aside all foolish things) and Wagner's *Gotterdam-
merung*. As Brunhilde sings with the flames of Valhalla illuminating her from behind:

"All things! All things! All is clear to me now!"

But that is only one part of von Trier's Wagnerian fantasy.
This is *Tristan*, not the *Ring*.

Melancholia's debt to Wagner was only superficially understood
in popular commentary. Most critics seemed to assume that
von Trier simply used Wagner's music to create a mood. It's just
a film score. Background music. *Annoying* background music.
As Dana Stevens contended in a *Slate* review of November 11,
2011: "The Wagner cue . . . struck me as a little much the first
time it was used; by the fourth, fifth, sixth time it was border-
ing on risible."

Actually, I think von Trier's use of the music is appropriately Wagnerian. It's a *leitmotif*. Early in the film, the music
is obscurely ominous. Later, it becomes clear that this ominousness is the ominousness of the rogue planet itself; the
music is the rogue planet's leitmotif. When the music returns,
we know that the planet is returning as our central concern.
The two, the music and the planet, come back persistently, as
if they were Beethoven's four note "fate motive" in the Fifth
Symphony. They return whether you think they're "risible" or

"a bit much" or not. Even the characters think it's a bit much. They seem to think, "Maybe if I look again it will be gone." But then, "That again! Is this real?" Again and again, the music, the planet. They are not going away. They are the insistence, like Beethoven's knock at the door, of the Real. All of the self-seeking vanities of humans are overwhelmed by the Revenge of the Material, the unrelenting planet.

The worst thing is that if you think that the *Tristan* overture is just music that von Trier happened to choose because he needed a film score and, hey, this sounds pretty good, you miss all the other ways in which the film is Wagnerian. The great theme of *Tristan und Isolde* is *liebestod*, or love/death. *Liebestod* is Wagner's version of the romantic project to resolve or harmonize the opposition of the subjective and objective. As Schelling asked, ". . . how does intelligence come to be added to nature?" How do knowledge and the object of knowledge become one thing? For Wagner this question becomes "how does the subjectivity of love resolve the denial of love that is in the loved one's betrayal, in grim nature, in social convention, and, ultimately, in the explicitness of death (the finite)?"*

For Wagner the answer to Schelling's question is in finding that love achieves its infinity, its perfection, in death itself. *Liebestod* transcends the opposition of love and death. Wagner

---

* For Schelling, this was *the* question of philosophy. He writes, "the whole of theoretical philosophy has this problem only to solve, namely how the restriction becomes ideal." Put in Wagnerian terms, the fundamental question of philosophy is how death (restriction) becomes love (the ideal).

deconstructs the opposition, finding them mutually dependent in both origin and destination. Of course, what makes Tristan's faith plausible to the opera's audience is not my prose translation of the idea but—and this is as it should be—the power of Wagner's music. The amazing satisfaction of the music of the third act of *Tristan* confirms *liebestod* in a way that any dramatic ambiguity cannot challenge. The music creates the world's "ought"; this is how the opposition of subject and object *ought* to be resolved, even if that resolution is, as Yeats put it, only the "artifice of eternity."

It is revealing that von Trier allows Justine to stage, to make theatrical, their deaths. This is remarkable because Justine has just finished telling Claire that her version of apocalyptic theater is a piece of shit. Justine's theater, apparently, is good shit. Why?

In that last moment Justine ceases to be "Aunt Deal-Breaker" (in the boy's words) and becomes Aunt Promise-Keeper. Justine does not conclude by saying, "See? I told you so! Evil! The world is evil! I'm glad it's ending! Good riddance!" No, she ends in creative play. That fact is crucially important to any adequate reading of the film. She and the boy spend their last moments gathering sticks to make a "magic cave," suggestive of so many of Wagner's enchanted places, but especially of the cave in *Siegfried* where the dwarf Mime raised Siegfried, and Siegfried became the heroic bearer of a magic sword. This cave is not merely Justine's effort to calm a little boy who might otherwise freak out. In its relation to the movie's other great movements it is an affirmation, an affirmation of the only place where the consolation of *liebestod* makes sense: in *art*, Nietzsche's "healing enchantress." In the cave, Justine is herself transformed, beyond illusion and beyond the despair that follows the end of illusion. She abandons her Self, the Self that has writhed in manic despair for the length of the movie, and discovers compassion for the suffering of others.

Once in their magic cave, yet another layer of complexity is added to the film. The faces of the characters express something Buddhistic, especially the boy who seems to be sitting in *zazen*, his eyes closed. This moment was anticipated briefly earlier in the film, in a moment that seemed almost gratuitous at the time, when Justine looked out of her bedroom window and saw her depressed mother assuming a yoga pose while looking out at the evening sky and, whether she knew it or not, the approaching planet.

Von Trier's trust is placed in art but also in that gesture that Buddhism calls "putting on your original face." Sitting in their magic cave, the three experience a sort of "sudden enlightenment" in which they are cleansed of passions (both joy and despair), desire, and hope. They discover charity. As the Chinese monk Lin Chi wrote in the ninth century: "To practice charity is to give everything away. This means to get rid of perceptions of self, being, life and soul, sorrow and delusion, possession and renunciation, love and hate." At the last possible moment, they give themselves away. This is neither a happy ending nor a sad ending. Our characters put on their original face and become part of what is. The dominant mood is simply *clarity*. They are at last awake. To paraphrase Flannery O'Connor: "They would have been wise if there had been a planet to destroy them every minute of their lives."

THE ART-BOT CAN'T DO THIS

"Art models freedom," said Schiller in 1795. Taking Schiller very literally, Delacroix offered his iconic "Liberty Leading the People" (1831) to the Paris Salon. The French state bought the painting but then, shortly thereafter, refused to display it because it was "inflammatory."

But doesn't this painting actually betray Schiller's idea about what art does? Can this be the freedom he had in mind? Doesn't Delacroix betray Schiller's freedom by *thematizing* it? There is a layer of conceptual dirt on this painting, a darkening of the veneer, that is difficult to look beyond. The painting has been so taken up by popular culture that one looks at it as if it were the product of a Disney studio. It presents only a cartoon freedom. Is *Liberty*, too, about the kitschy degeneration of painting as with Runge's painting *The Huelsenbeck Children*? Does Delacroix cheapen Schiller?

What are we to make of the soft-core perfection of Liberty's exposed breasts? It's as if Delacroix got confused and thought he was that very different kind of painter of the period (like his bitter enemy Ingres's *Odalisque*) who asks the model to recline on a couch, smallish, conical breasts glowing, a mirror just behind to catch the cleft of her ass, and a couple of monkeys rubbing themselves raw on the armrests.

But wait, there is another and very incongruous thing that demands the eye (beyond said breasts): a sad but luminous gray-blue sock on a corpse. These socks thrust up practically into the center of the painting. Liberty might trip over them in her next step through the corpses. His pants have been pilfered and one sock is gone (the vultures of war must have been in a hurry), but the remaining sock is bunched at his ankle and looks slovenly, sordid, and hopeless. Doesn't this sock argue against the painting's most apparent claim? Doesn't it save the painting from its own sincerity? Such a great, heroic, deluded dream undone by a sock!

Or is it perhaps the case that this pathetic sock is simply an *homage* to a painting that made such a tremendous impression on Delacroix that "he went running like a madman": Gericault's *The Raft of the Medusa*. Here, too, at the margin of the central drama a bathetic sock falls from a foot (lower left corner) its owner also deprived of his pants.

How could Delacroix not have been thinking of Gericault as he painted his sock? He knew every inch of *The Raft*, every brush stroke. And if he was thinking of Gericault, how could he be taking entirely seriously the drama he was staging? "I'm not for this sort of simpleton's revolution," he might be saying, "I'm performing a familiar dramatic set piece (it's not about

Revolution!) and I've underlined that fact with Gericault's sock! My real interest is elsewhere, in something the mob, the common man, would never suspect."

Delacroix himself was no revolutionary. He wrote in his famous *Journal*, "1848. The liberty won at the cost of battles is not really liberty at all." He wasn't even all that fond of humans, especially in masses. He was Nietzschean before the fact. On the other hand, he *was* fond of energy, light, and color. Leave the dubious celebrations of revolutionary zeal to Jacques-Louis David and his school of painterly propagandists, as in David's *Napoleon Crossing the Alps* (below) or as in Bartholdi's *Liberty Enlightening the World* (better known to us as the Statue of Liberty) inspired by Delacroix's painting.*

No dirty socks here, and no irony.

---

* The Statue of Liberty: the world's largest work of sentimental bric-a-brac.

There is a deeply serious intent in *Liberty*, one that affirms Schiller's idea about the relationship of art and freedom, but this intent is not in an image of a topless lady with a flag. What affirms Schiller is something we hardly see at all: the painting's arc of energy. Beginning with the foundation of corpses at the base of the painting, Delacroix initiates a bold, earthy sweep to the left, as if a wave were gathering massive energy that will be played out later in many smaller gestures and events. This energy is taken up by the figures behind Liberty, all of whom are looking to their left, their swords and rifles rising up to the clouds, as if they formed the crest of a wave which, in the moment after this image, will crash down and clear the past away leaving only a barren stretch of sand. This, too, is something that Delacroix learned from Gericault, whose raft surges upwards with such energy that it seems about to fly. And what is at the leading edge of the raft's energy? A hand lifted and waving not the *tricolor* but a dirty shirt.

So which is it? This painting is either a capitulation to political sentimentality or it is the subtle demolition of that sentimentality. As Delacroix wrote in his journal: "You [bourgeois] live like wolves and your arts are doves." *Liberty Leading the People* is taken for dove art by its millions of admirers when what it wants to be is an apocalypse. That it became a piece of liberal kitsch used most often to celebrate bourgeois revolutions is a cruel piece of inattention.

Liberty is a Romantic painting, and not the piece of propaganda it appears to be, because it is spiritually a *landscape* concerned with that helix of energy that the Romantics called Nature. Nature takes up and belittles the delusions of human action even when this action is on the grandest scale. Beyond that is only the sound of pistols, the fury of bodies driven before the wind, just the sort of futility that drove Delacroix into fits of ennui.

This painting is in a code that the Art-Bot can't understand. Nothing in my reading of the painting makes it worth hundreds of millions of dollars to arid and acidic art speculators. More, my idea that two of the most famous images in the history of art can be interpreted through dirty, crumpled socks makes me laugh a Rabelaisian laugh. *My reading may not be true but it is alive*, and that is something entirely missing in a world designed for the convenience of the Money-Bot.

My reading laughs because, like Schiller and Delacroix, I too would like people to be free.

SUFJAN STEVENS'S VENGEFUL PLAY

I was listening to Sufjan Stevens's song "I Walked" on his album *The Age of Adz* when it occurred to me how much in keeping his work is with the project of Romanticism. Like the Romantics, Stevens is alienated from the values of the culture into which he happened to be born. He is so alienated from them that it doesn't occur to him to rebel; rather, it is as if he has simply never heard of that culture. He says, "America? Christianity? Sorry, I'm from Adz. Things are arranged differently there." This is the Romantic strategy par excellence: not a confrontation but a purposeful wandering away from the oppressive reason for alienation. Like William Blake, Stevens creates his own religion in order not to be condemned to another's. As the song announces, "he walked." He's so *gone*, as the beatniks said.

In this, Stevens is both thoughtfully naive and innocently knowing. His work rests not only with Blake but with other straight-faced art-mystics who articulated their revolution with "gorgeous nonsense." The Cocteau Twins' explicitly nonsensical gorgeosity, Nina Hagen's Nun-Sex-Monk-Rock (the Antiworld of Cosma Shiva), Jimi Hendrix's *Axis: Bold as Love* ("Just ask the Axis, he knows everything"), George Clinton's *Mothership Connection*, and Sun Ra's "Gods of the Thunder Realm." If that's too pop for you, then Piet Mondrian's theosophical paintings like "Passion Flower" and "Devotion", William Butler Yeats's *A Vision* (The Subdivisions of the Wheel: Will, Mask, Creative Mind, Body of Fate), Caspar David Friedrich's "Mountain Landscape with Rainbow," Jacob Boehme's *De Signatura Rerum* ("if he has the Hammer that can strike my Bell!"), John's "Book of Revelation" (the Seventh Seal, the Wrath of the Lamb), the salvific Arcanum of the Gnostics, Plotinus's emanation of the Nous and World Soul, and, finally, Plato, nonsensical origin of all these blessedly daft spheres.

These are the folk what begat the folk what begat Sufjan

Stevens. Whether the mysticism of the spheres or a more mod-
ish mysticism of sci-fi alien contacts, the purpose of these traditions is to turn alienation on its head—it's the real world that
is alien—by revealing an unseen world that condemns conventional reality as a vast, enslaving fraud.

But what draws me inside Stevens's music is not its iconoclastic teaching but its harmonics. (For nature mystics, all of the
elaborate systems of Gnosis could be reduced to the right vibra-
tion or wavelength, the ringing of a bell.) The song "I Walked"
is accompanied by an icy-pure chorus of female voices. This
music is anything but avant-garde or even avant-pop; it is an
appeal back to the spiritual music that was once the Church's
proudest ornament: Palestrina or Bach or Handel. Like them,
the voices on *Adz* restore faith's "abstract purity" (Shelley).*
Disabused of the world's wisdom by the world itself, Stevens
creates his own world and "redeems from decay the visitations
of the divinity in man." (Shelley, "A Defense of Poetry") Like
Shelley, Stevens seeks to speak the divine through the artwork
and thus preserve it not as catechism or credo but as something
that could be *lived*, certainly lived for the duration of the work
itself, but also lived after as a kind of light blue wash over our
lives, art's promise of happiness. Against such an experience,
the world-as-it-happens-to-be looks poor. We experience the
real world as disenchantment. Art *longs* for a counter-world, be

---

* Every year Stevens and friends write and perform Christmas songs that feature choral
harmonies.

it a house full of English poets in Geneva in 1816 (parsing the numinous and telling each other stories about the monsters science makes), or an enclave of refuse-niks, playing guitar, reading Walt Whitman, cranking Beck's "Devil's Haircut," and in most other ways thriving just off Burnside near Powell's Bookstore in Portland, Oregon, circa 2015. Stevens delivers all this with the modesty of the folksinger. His primary message is: don't take this *too* seriously, just seriously enough that you can walk with me away from this world and into another.

This may seem as if I am glorifying Stevens in a way that his music will not support. And perhaps it is true that his music will not bear comparison to the music of Beethoven or Mahler. Well, assuming that's true (although I have my doubts about knee-jerk deference to the classical masters, especially with an artist like Stevens who uses minimalism so effectively in his pop and so explicitly in "Round Up," a work commissioned by the Brooklyn Academy of Music), so what? My point is not evaluative; my point is syntactic. My point is that the deep historical forces that make Stevens possible include Beethoven as well as Plato. Millions of (mostly) young people eagerly await the next album from of Montreal, Neutral Milk Hotel (if there ever is a next album), the Knife (sadly disbanded), the Animal Collective, 31 Knots, Run the Jewels, Deerhunter, Sonic Youth (very sadly disbanded), or (best band since the Beatles) Radiohead just so that they can be reminded again of what it feels like to be *alive*, and just so that they can be in touch with *something worth being loyal to.*

And that ain't nothin'.

The people who live this loyalty have gathered in cities like Brooklyn, San Francisco, Portland, and Seattle in order to be among their kind. It's their idea of church: "for where two or three are gathered together in my name, there am I in the midst of them." While they are happy to have their ad hoc urban congregations, where they try to live the Greek dream of the polis, they feel mostly helpless before the money system. So they work in local bookstores, organic groceries, or in bars and restaurants. They temp in local colleges or work for social welfare nonprofits. They stay in grad school as *long* as possible. Or they take it on the chin as the "useful smart person" who checks the investment banker's grammar and does other things that useful smart people do while feeling guilty and defeated by Necessity.

But their real life is lived in a word-of-mouth utopia greased by social media (even though they know at some level that Facebook and Google are not their friends). "You've got to hear this band," one says on Facebook, "they have a new album and they're playing downtown this weekend." It's a form of love, really. In giving me *The Age of Adz*, my daughter said, "I'm obsessed with this album." She thought I could be, too. If it enriched her inner life, she imagined generously that it could enrich mine. She gave it to me out of a desire that all beings should be happy. Especially her dad.

Now you might say that that's an easy thing for her to do, me being her father and all. But how common is this sort of scene? You see someone in an airport listening to her iPod. She's wearing some sub-culture cue, like a Modest Mouse T-shirt, a piercing, a streak of pink in her hair, a not-so-discreet tat, so you take a risk and ask what she's listening to. She says, "I'm listening to of Montreal's *Skeletal Lamping.*" You say, "That's a fucking great album." (You are both now bonded in some pleasant part of the posterior region of the cortex. If someone scanned your brains with magnetoencephalography at just that moment, it would look like you were having sex.) I mean, here you were on this shitty trip, in an airport, eating yet another doughnut, but now you're "cheerful." Remember Ian Drury and the Blockheads' "Reasons to Be Cheerful, Part 3"? The song's cunning is that the song itself is the main reason to be cheerful, not his comical list of things ("Bantu Steven Biko, listening to Reko/Harpo Groucho Chico"). You feel as if you have just participated in something that was one part recruitment for a revolution and one part wisdom event. Most importantly, you come away feeling happy and alive.

This loyalty through art is very different from loyalty to a political party, or movement, or struggle. The counterculture of art reclaims the right to pleasure and play *now* and not in some distant time when socialism has made the world right. Dress up now, put on the funky feathers and beads now, dance now, fuck now, laugh a lot, have friends now. Be happy right now! So, it's a word-of-mouth utopia, but it's also a refusal of the mass loneliness overseen by the Money-Bot.

A counterculture is an appeal to the idea that reforming institutions and political organizations is never enough. We have had our experiences with revolutions seeking better institutions and laws, and we should know now that they have been in every case insufficient and, more often than not, disappointing and destructive. This is not to say that reformed institutions are not desirable; it is only to say that they are *not enough*. In the West, art has provided us with something more than social revolution, something that goes beyond this or that "party line." Since the Romantics, art and artists have encouraged us to *live differently*. With its emphasis on change and creativity, Buddhism offers something similar. As David Loy writes in *A New Buddhist Path*, "Buddhism offers an alternative approach: the path is really about personal transformation . . . not to qualify for a blissful afterlife but to live in a different way here and now."

When Morse Peckham said that Romanticism was the greatest event in human history since the founding of the first cities, he had reasons.* With Romanticism, the West had for the first time a new kind of internal dissonance. People now lived in a doubled world, one bluntly oppressive and dull, the other full of the promise of freedom and life. Romanticism was a powerful appeal to ordinary people to walk away from the world as it is into something new, more human, and more like nature. The current music-driven counter-world is not the expression of some uniquely contemporary genius. It is not the arrival at

---

* I've referred to Peckham several times now, and I spend considerable time discussing him in my earlier book *The Science Delusion*. His book *Romanticism: The Culture of the Nineteenth Century* completely reoriented my thinking about Romantic art. His emphasis was on Romanticism as, first, a social movement, the origin of the idea of artists as alienated subjects in search of an alternative world more in keeping with their feelings and ideas.

last of the Answer, and it is certainly not new. It is simply the most recent form of Romanticism's Great Yeah to Life.

That's all and that's enough.

•

"If I was walking around somewhere, on the street, it was in-stant tribal identification," says Ian MacKaye. "I'd see people and immediately be attracted to them—some woman with a shaved head or just something about them, it was just instant identification. And it was really a very important aspect of my community and the larger community that I felt a part of."
—QUOTED IN *Our Band Could Be Your Life: Scenes from the American Indie Underground 1981–1991* BY MICHAEL AZERRAD

•

SOMETHING WORTH BEING LOYAL TO

As I was listening to the chorus of women on "I Walked," I thought to myself, "These sweetly gathered voices are individ-ual women. I wonder who they are. Friends of Sufjan's? Session singers at microscopic Asthmatic Kitty Records?" (Asthmatic Kitty! Come on! That's great! Buñuel couldn't have done bet-ter. Can't you imagine the inventory he'd make of all the differ-ent types of kitties? The Discrete Kitty. The Kitty of Malicious Intent. The Kitty of the Noon Wine. Etc.)

Every one of these voices comes from a real woman with her own damaged tale to tell. Thus for an imaginable one of them: her parents divorced when she was five, she moved with her mother into poverty and into Grandma's two-bedroom duplex, she was molested by the son of one of her mother's cousins, she got slapped some for the crime of being a teenager, she banged her nose against the clear glass door of depression ("What the fuck is this? What the fuck is wrong with me?"), she got various piercings and tats, she was discovered one morning plunging a steak knife into her mattress (her Goth mascara made her cheeks a morbid and joyless batik), she plunged the knife for no reason other than unrefined teenage misery, she got more tats, she excelled in college in spite of it all, and ended with a Masters degree in something helpful to others. Most importantly, she was saved moment-by-moment in her life by music, which offered the kindness of a tiny bead of dopamine dripped down from her congested neurotransmitters. But forget that, the music she heard was so beautiful that it made her cry a certain kind of transcendental tear. At last, she discovered that what she wanted was to be more intimately one with this music. She wanted to sing.

It didn't matter that she paid rent by waiting tables and flashing her *gluteus maximus* at *Que Guapa!*, the swank tapas bar out in the U-District by the lake. Didn't matter that when she complained about the little skirt she had to wear (a skirt that did more shading than clothing of said glutes), Julio, the lecherous manager with the doo-wop hair, excused the skirt by saying, "*Por supuesto*, but it's so very Latin!" Then he'd yank at his crotch as if to say, "Now you understand and we can stop having this conversation and not have it ever again because I've made it so clear that there is no point. You're wearing the skirt." Didn't matter that she drove a rusted Mazda Protégé with a treated pine 2x6 for a bumper. Didn't matter. Didn't matter because that's how it had to go in order to come together with her friends and create this perfect, crystalline distillation of me-ness/us-ness, this moment that is recorded on track one, side B of the vinyl version of *The Age of Adz*.*

But then, contradictorily, I thought that the voice of these girls was completely impersonal, and had nothing to do with any sad teenage tales. What the girls were about was something beyond them. Call it a liquid distillation of eternity. They were part of what Johann Fichte called the true human "vocation," known intuitively through a "voice inside of me" that says: "You are free. Live like it."

The world is irredeemable, but that sound, that note, that music is vengeful play. It doesn't need a revolution or, God help us, the feeble triumph of a Democratic president, because it already *is* the world it wants. It is the music not only of spheres but of all of us who choose to live in the counter-world.

---

* The perfecting of the unity of subject and object, the "I" thriving in the context of a fully realized human community, is one of Romanticism's oldest themes. Example: in the first section of Beethoven's *Missa Solemnis*, listen to how the powerful individual voices— soprano, tenor, bass, each in turn—arise from the massed body of the chorus like finely articulated spirits from the depth of the earth.

ACKNOWLEDGMENTS

Heartfelt thanks to Kelly Burdick, Andrew Cooper, Linda Heuman, David Loy, Donald Lopez, Lewis Lapham, and Leopold Froelich.

NOTES

1. *The Discourse on Voluntary Servitude*, 1552. Boétie was the first to recognize that, contra Machiavelli, fear was not sufficient for a monarch to remain in power, and that people had to be led to consent to their own domination.
2. According to a 2013 study by Oxford economists, 47 percent of remaining American jobs are susceptible to automation, especially low-paying jobs in the food industry. ("The Future of Employment: How Susceptible Are Jobs to Computerisation?" Frey and Osborne, September 17, 2013.)
3. Agamben is thinking of concentration camps where the "bare life" of prisoners leaves the "state of exception" (the state of being an exception to social norms) and becomes a norm.
4. See Michael Katz's *The Undeserving Poor* (1990).
5. See also "Household Finances May Curb Holiday Spending," Hiroko Tabuchi, *The New York Times*, October 14, 2014. Tabuchi observes that in the coming holiday season retailers like Kmart might find it difficult to get middle-income shoppers to spend more. "Stagnant wage growth, coupled with the rising costs of health care, child care, housing and other essentials, means that many American simply have less money left at the end of the year for presents, experts say. Reflecting imbalances elsewhere in the economy, much of the holiday season spending will come from wealthier shoppers." The most visible sign of this erosion of consumption is the demise of the middle-class shopping mall with Sears and J.C. Penney's anchoring the north and south ends. (For grisly details, see the website Deadmalls.com.)

6. See Robert Putnam, *Our Kids: The American Dream in Crisis*, 2015, for a full presentation of the failures of public education.

7. See Christopher Breu's book *Insistence of the Material* (2014) for a full exposition of this fantasy.

8. This essay is adapted from the chapter "Free Will" in his book *The Meaning of Human Existence* (2014).

9. See also Jonathan Gottschall's *The Storytelling Animal*, in which Gottschall encourages his reader to think that story is about "how a set of brain circuits . . . force narrative structure on the chaos of our lives."

10. "As we know, in the Oriental systems, principally in Buddhism, *nothing* is the absolute principle" (Hegel, *Science of Logic*). The Buddhist concept that Hegel is most likely referring to is *sunyata*, or emptiness. *Sunyata* is better understood as *unlimited potentiality*, not the void. As David Loy puts it, *sunyata* is "a metaphor for the irreducible dynamic creativity of the cosmos, ceaselessly generating new forms out of itself."

11. See, for example, Ronald D. Siegel's book *The Mindfulness Solution* or his Teaching Company lectures, *The Science of Mindfulness: A Research-Based Path to Well-Being*, in which students are encouraged to "study the brain science underlying these traditional wisdom practices."

12. See Jeffrey St. Clair's *Been Brown So Long It Looked Like Green to Me: The Politics of Nature* (2004).

13. See Eugenia Williamson's essay "PBS Self-Destructs," *Harper's Magazine*, October 2014.

14. See also John Gardner's *On Moral Fiction* (1979) and Charles Newman's *The Postmodern Aura* (1985).